CW00549891

GCSE
Success

Additional Science

Carla Newman
Joanne Barton
John Sadler
Jon Dwyer
Colin Porter
Charles Cotton

Contents

Chemistry

Revised

Contents

3

Cells and Organisation

Biology

Multiple-choice questions

Choose just one answer: A, B, C or D.

1. Which of these would only be found in a plant cell? **(1 mark)**
   - **A** mitochondria
   - **B** cell wall
   - **C** cell membrane
   - **D** cytoplasm

2. Which of these is a pigment used in photosynthesis? **(1 mark)**
   - **A** cytoplasm
   - **B** chloroplasts
   - **C** chlorophyll
   - **D** cellulose

3. Which of these structures is the smallest? **(1 mark)**
   - **A** cell wall
   - **B** nucleus

   - **C** cytoplasm
   - **D** mitochondria

4. Organisms which are able to exist in isolation are known as **(1 mark)**
   - **A** unicellular
   - **B** multicellular
   - **C** tissues
   - **D** organ systems

5. Bacteria belong to which large group of organisms? **(1 mark)**
   - **A** mammals
   - **B** prokaryotes
   - **C** eukaryotes
   - **D** invertebrates

Score / 5

Short-answer questions

1. **True or false?** | True | False | (9 marks)

   a) An electron microscope can resolve smaller objects than a light microscope. ☐ ☐

   b) The human eye can resolve smaller objects than a light microscope. ☐ ☐

   c) Mitochondria can be seen with a light microscope. ☐ ☐

   d) A plant cell vacuole can be seen with a light microscope. ☐ ☐

   e) Ribosomes can be seen with an electron microscope. ☐ ☐

   f) Electron microscopes can resolve structures at around 0.002 mm. ☐ ☐

   g) A tissue is bigger than a cell. ☐ ☐

   h) Xylem is an example of a tissue. ☐ ☐

   i) A heart is an example of an organ. ☐ ☐

Score / 9

Answer all parts of all questions. Continue on a separate sheet of paper if necessary.

1 a) Identify which is an animal cell and which is a plant cell on the diagram captions. **(2 marks)**

b) Complete the labels on the diagrams. **(12 marks)**

1 .... cell   2 .... cell

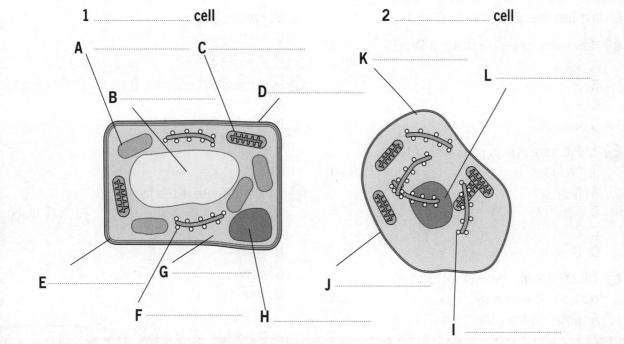

c) Describe the role of mitochondria, chloroplasts and cytoplasm in the cell. **(3 marks)**

....

....

....

2 Is a muscle a tissue or an organ? Explain your answer. **(2 marks)**

....

....

3 Name three difficulties of being multicellular which unicellular organisms would not experience. **(3 marks)**

....

....

....

....

Score   / 22

Biology

How well did you do?

| 0–9 | Try again | 10–18 | Getting there | 19–27 | Good work | 28–36 | Excellent! |

For more information on this topic, see pages 4–5 of your Success Revision Guide.

5

DNA and Protein Synthesis

Multiple-choice questions

Choose just one answer: A, B, C or D.

1 How many bases are there in DNA? **(1 mark)**
- **A** 1
- **B** 2
- **C** 3
- **D** 4

2 Which base always pairs with 'A' in DNA? **(1 mark)**
- **A** A
- **B** T
- **C** C
- **D** G

3 Which scientist did not focus their work on DNA directly? **(1 mark)**
- **A** Rosalind Franklin
- **B** Erwin Chargaff
- **C** Charles Darwin
- **D** Frances Crick

4 How many strands does DNA have? **(1 mark)**
- **A** 1
- **B** 2
- **C** 3
- **D** 4

5 Which of these is the largest structure? **(1 mark)**
- **A** DNA
- **B** gene
- **C** base
- **D** triplet code

Score   / 5

Short-answer questions

1
a) What is a sequence of three bases known as? .... **(1 mark)**

b) How many amino acids would these three bases code for? .... **(1 mark)**

c) What is the name of the process whereby amino acids are identified by the

code and joined to make a polypeptide (protein)? .... **(1 mark)**

d) What molecule 'reads' the code and conducts the process of adding amino acids? **(1 mark)**

....

e) Where does translation happen? .... **(1 mark)**

f) Name the difference between DNA and mRNA. .... **(1 mark)**

....

2 **True or false?**

	True	False	
a) The evidence for DNA structure came from microscope images.	☐	☐	**(1 mark)**
b) Maurice Wilkins and Rosalind Franklin used X-rays to investigate DNA structure.	☐	☐	**(1 mark)**
c) Watson and Crick were responsible for suggesting that DNA has a double helix structure.	☐	☐	**(1 mark)**

Score   / 9

Answer all parts of all questions. Continue on a separate sheet of paper if necessary.

❶ In what order do these events happen to synthesise a protein? (6 marks)

A	Section of DNA containing a gene 'unzips'.
B	mRNA forms a single stranded DNA template (transcription).
C	Triplet codes of bases on the new strand are 'read' by tRNA and ribosomes (translation).
D	Ribosomes add amino acids according to the triplet code.
E	mRNA moves out of nucleus to the cytoplasm.
F	Amino acids form a (polypeptide) protein.
G	Free bases (on tRNA) pair with mRNA strand.

ANSWER:

A						

❷ Why can mRNA leave the nucleus but DNA cannot? (1 mark)

❸ Which of these is not made of protein? (Tick the box.) (1 mark)

DNA
enzymes
haemoglobin
cell wall (in a plant)

❹ What is meant by the term helix? .... (1 mark)

❺ What substances make up the two 'backbone' strands of the helix? (2 marks)

❻ Arrange the following in order of magnitude from the largest to the smallest. (4 marks)

chromosome   **base**   **protein**   **gene**

.... ⟶ .... ⟶ .... ⟶ ....

Score   / 15

How well did you do?

| 0–7 | Try again | 8–14 | Getting there | 15–21 | Good work | 22–29 | Excellent! |

For more information on this topic, see pages 6–7 of your Success Revision Guide.

7

Biology

Proteins and Enzymes

Multiple-choice questions

Choose just one answer: A, B, C or D.

1 The optimum temperature for enzymes that work in the human body is **(1 mark)**
- **A** 27 °C
- **B** 37 °C
- **C** 47 °C
- **D** 57 °C

2 Which temperature is likely to produce the lowest rate of reaction for respiration in humans? **(1 mark)**
- **A** 27 °C
- **B** 37 °C
- **C** 47 °C
- **D** 57 °C

3 What is the name of the part of the enzyme where the substrate fits into the molecule? **(1 mark)**
- **A** active immunity
- **B** active site
- **C** active revision
- **D** active area

4 Heat changes the shape of the enzyme molecule. When this happens we say that the enzyme has been **(1 mark)**
- **A** killed
- **B** denatured
- **C** melted
- **D** squashed

5 The molecule that the enzyme works on is known as the **(1 mark)**
- **A** substitute
- **B** reactant
- **C** product
- **D** substrate

Score / 5

Short-answer questions

1 Name three processes that use enzymes. (3 marks)

2 Give four uses of proteins in the body and give an example for each. (4 marks)

3 'Biological' washing powder contains enzymes used by our bodies to digest food.

a) Why are enzymes included in the washing powder? (1 mark)

b) If you are using 'biological' washing powder, the manufacturers recommend a maximum washing temperature of 40 °C. Explain why this is. (2 marks)

Score / 10

Answer all parts of all questions. Continue on a separate sheet of paper if necessary.

① Protein is a polymer (a long chain molecule made of many repeating sub-units).

What are the sub-units of the protein polymer? .... (1 mark)

② **a)** What is meant by the term 'biological catalyst'? (2 marks)

....

....

b) What name is given to biological catalysts working in the body? .... (1 mark)

③

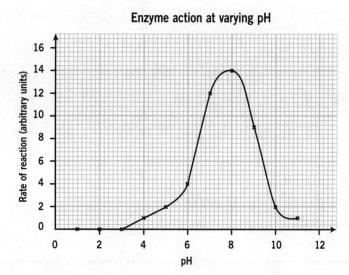

Enzyme action at varying pH

a) What is the optimum pH for this particular enzyme? .... (1 mark)

b) Give an example of a place in the human body where this enzyme might work well. (1 mark)

....

c) What has happened to the enzymes at pH 2? .... (1 mark)

d) Describe what this means in terms of the enzyme's structure. (2 marks)

....

....

e) Why is enzyme action sometimes likened to a lock and key? (2 marks)

....

....

....

Score   / 11

Biology

How well did you do?

| 0–6 | Try again | 7–13 | Getting there | 14–19 | Good work | 20–26 | Excellent! |

For more information on this topic, see pages 8–9 of your Success Revision Guide.

Cell Division

Multiple-choice questions

Choose just one answer: A, B, C or D.

1 Which of these is a type of cell division? **(1 mark)**
- **A** haploid
- **B** diploid
- **C** mitosis
- **D** mutation

2 Which of these is unlikely to cause a genetic mutation? **(1 mark)**
- **A** UV in sunlight
- **B** X-rays
- **C** ultrasound
- **D** chemical mutagens

3 Which of these does not result in variation in the offspring? **(1 mark)**
- **A** random pairing of parents
- **B** mutations in the genes
- **C** asexual reproduction
- **D** formation of gametes

4 How many cells are produced by mitotic cell division? **(1 mark)**
- **A** 1
- **B** 2
- **C** 3
- **D** 4

5 How many cells are produced by meiotic cell division? **(1 mark)**
- **A** 1
- **B** 2
- **C** 3
- **D** 4

Score   / 5

Short-answer questions

1 a) What word describes a cell that has only one copy of each of its chromosomes?   **(1 mark)**

b) What name is given to these cells? ....   **(1 mark)**

c) What name is given to the process whereby two of these cells fuse?   **(1 mark)**

d) What type of reproduction involves this process? ....   **(1 mark)**

2 Fill in the gaps in the paragraph below using these words.   **(7 marks)**

| gene | DNA | variation | changes | proteins | insignificant | mutations |

Mutations can bring about changes to the .... of an organism. Sometimes this results

in a new .... being formed, meaning that the cell can make new ....

This might be an advantage for the organism because it produces .... Usually

though, ... make such small .... to the DNA that they

are .... in changing the gene.

Score   / 11

Answer all parts of all questions. Continue on a separate sheet of paper if necessary.

1 a) What is the diploid number in human body cells? (1 mark)

....

b) What number of chromosomes would you find in a sperm cell? (1 mark)

....

c) The cells of which tissue type make sperm cells? (1 mark)

....

d) Which type of cell division is responsible for making the sperm? (1 mark)

....

e) Give one advantage of sexual reproduction over asexual reproduction. (1 mark)

....

2 What is the sequence of these events in meiosis? (5 marks)

A	Paired chromosomes separate.
B	Two cells are formed.
C	To form a total of four, new, haploid cells.
D	DNA becomes organised into chromosome pairs.
E	Each double stranded chromosome now separates.
F	DNA is copied.

F					

3 Mutation plays a great part in the evolution of strains of bacteria.
Explain how using antibacterial surface wipes could assist this process. (5 marks)

....

....

....

....

Score   / 15

Biology

How well did you do?

| 0–7 | Try again | 8–15 | Getting there | 16–23 | Good work | 24–31 | Excellent! |

For more information on this topic, see pages 10–11 of your Success Revision Guide.

Growth and Development

Multiple-choice questions

Choose just one answer: A, B, C or D.

1 Which of these is NOT a plant organ? **(1 mark)**
- **A** root
- **B** stem
- **C** leaf
- **D** xylem

2 What word do we use to describe genetically identical organisms? **(1 mark)**
- **A** zygotes
- **B** clones
- **C** copies
- **D** gametes

3 What word would accurately describe a stem cell? **(1 mark)**
- **A** specialised
- **B** universal
- **C** stalks
- **D** undifferentiated

4 What word describes the cell formed by fertilisation of gametes? **(1 mark)**
- **A** zygote
- **B** clone
- **C** copy
- **D** gamete

5 Areas of a plant where cells are undifferentiated are known as **(1 mark)**
- **A** hapistems
- **B** useful
- **C** meristems
- **D** stalks

Score   / 5

Short-answer questions

1 Match these keywords with their definitions. (6 marks)

gene switching	fertilised egg in the early stages of development
gamete	specialised for a specific job – not all genes switched on
differentiated	sex cell e.g. sperm or egg, pollen or ovule
embryo	ability to stop expression of some genes in favour of others
embryonic stem cell	completely unspecialised cell taken before the eight cell stage of an embryo or found in umbilical cord blood
stem cell	unspecialised cell which has all the genes present in its nucleus switched on

2 Which of these are potential uses for stem cells? Tick all that apply. (1 mark)

☐ To generate insulin – producing cells for diabetes sufferers so they don't have to inject insulin

☐ To re-grow damaged nerve tissue in patients which have had accidents and severed nerves

☐ To grow new organs for transplant

Score   / 7

GCSE-style questions

Answer all parts of all questions. Continue on a separate sheet of paper if necessary.

1 Look at the opinions about stem cell research.

Mark: Stem cell research should be banned. It is not right to interfere with nature like this.

Erica: Stem cell research is expensive. We can save more lives by investing in vaccines.

Javelle: Stem cells could potentially save and improve many lives by replacing ineffective or damaged tissue.

Ella: We need to look into the risks before we use cloned stem cells in humans.

a) Who has suggested a use for stem cells that might justify investment in research? **(1 mark)**

b) Who has made a comment based on ethical reasons? **(1 mark)**

c) Who is exercising the precautionary principle in their attitude to stem

cell research? **(1 mark)**

2 a) Order these steps to producing measurements of dry mass for the mushrooms growing on a square metre of land. **(5 marks)**

A The mass of these mushrooms is measured.

B An area of 1 m² is chosen at random from a field (either by sampling with a quadrat or grid sampling).

C The mushrooms are removed from the oven and their mass is re-measured.

D The mushrooms in this area are picked.

E The mushrooms are placed in a warm oven for an hour.

F The mass is compared to the last measurement of mass taken.

G The process is repeated, returning the mushrooms to the oven and reweighing them alternately until no further loss of mass is recorded.

						G

b) What type of biomass is measured in step 'A' above? **(1 mark)**

c) What is the purpose of step G? **(1 mark)**

Score   / 10

How well did you do?

| 0–5 | Try again | 6–11 | Getting there | 12–17 | Good work | 18–22 | Excellent! |

For more information on this topic, see pages 12–13 of your Success Revision Guide.

Biology

Transport in Cells

Biology

Multiple-choice questions

Choose just one answer: A, B, C or D.

1 Which of these is NOT the name of
a method of transport in cells? **(1 mark)**
   A active transport
   B passive transport
   C diffusion
   D osmosis

2 Which of these words would NOT
accurately describe diffusion? **(1 mark)**
   A deliberate
   B passive
   C down a concentration gradient
   D random

3 Which of these is a special case of diffusion
relating to the movement of water? **(1 mark)**
   A osmosis
   B active transport
   C flaccid
   D turgid

4 Which of these describes a plant cell
that has lost much of its cellular
water, causing it to shrink? **(1 mark)**
   A plasmolysed
   B dry
   C turgid
   D arid

5 Which of these best describes a
plant whose cells have lost a
significant amount of water? **(1 mark)**
   A turgid
   B flaccid
   C wilted
   D arid

Score / 5

Short-answer questions

1 Add these labels in the correct place on the diagram. (7 marks)

cell   oxygen   cell   glucose   carbon dioxide
waste chemicals   blood capillaries

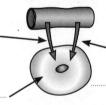 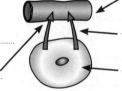

2 For each of the substances below, identify if it moves between the tissues and
bloodstream by osmosis or by diffusion. (5 marks)

   a) glucose ....   b) oxygen ....

   c) urea ....   d) water ....

   e) carbon dioxide ....

Score / 12

Answer all parts of all questions. Continue on a separate sheet of paper if necessary.

1 Farmers add fertiliser to the soil to ensure plants have the minerals they need to make maximum growth. Explain what might happen to their crops if they add too much fertiliser to the soil. (Answer on a separate sheet of paper.) **(4 marks)**

2 Explain what might happen to red blood cells when placed in a solution of pure water. (Answer on a separate sheet of paper.) **(5 marks)**

3 The graph below shows the % change in mass of potato pieces which have been submerged in sugar solutions of varying concentration for 1 hour. Use this graph and your knowledge of osmosis to answer the questions.

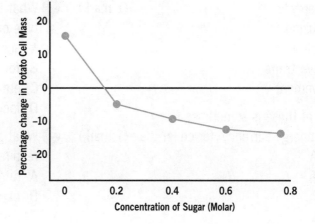

a) i) Describe what you might expect to happen to the potato if left in 0.2M sugar solution for another 2 hours. **(2 marks)**

....

....

ii) Explain why this would happen. **(2 marks)**

....

....

b) Estimate the concentration of the sugar solution inside the potato. .... **(1 mark)**

c) i) Describe what you would expect to happen if you submerged the potato pieces in sugar solutions of higher concentration than 0.8M. **(1 mark)**

....

....

ii) Explain why this would happen. **(2 marks)**

....

....

Score   / 17

How well did you do?

| 0–8 | Try again | 9–16 | Getting there | 17–25 | Good work | 26–34 | Excellent! |

For more information on this topic, see pages 14–15 of your Success Revision Guide.

Biology

Respiration

Multiple-choice questions

Choose just one answer: A, B, C or D.

1 Which of these processes does not use energy? **(1 mark)**
- **A** diffusion
- **B** respiration
- **C** active transport
- **D** movement

2 Which of these is sometimes know as an 'energy currency' for cells? **(1 mark)**
- **A** DNA
- **B** RNA
- **C** ATP
- **D** LOL

3 What type of respiration produces acid in human cells? **(1 mark)**
- **A** aerobic
- **B** anaerobic
- **C** energetic
- **D** diabolic

4 What is the acid produced in the type of respiration in question 3? **(1 mark)**
- **A** acetic
- **B** folic
- **C** ethanoic
- **D** lactic

5 What gas is produced by aerobic respiration? **(1 mark)**
- **A** nitrogen
- **B** oxygen
- **C** carbon monoxide
- **D** carbon dioxide

Score   / 5

Short-answer questions

1 Complete the table, ticking (✓) all boxes that apply in each row. **(5 marks)**

Substance	Product of aerobic respiration	Product of anaerobic respiration
glucose		
carbon dioxide		
lactic acid		
energy		
water		
oxygen		

2 a) Anaerobic respiration in yeast is usefully used in industry. What is this process known as? .... **(1 mark)**

b) Which product of this process is used in bread making? .... **(1 mark)**

c) Which product of this process is used in beer making? .... **(1 mark)**

Score   / 8

GCSE-style questions

Answer all parts of all questions. Continue on a separate sheet of paper if necessary.

1 ✎ Athletes completing a race continue to breathe heavily after the end of the race. Explain what causes this to be necessary. (Answer on a separate sheet of paper.) **(6 marks)**

2 a) What warning signal does the body receive to prevent exercise from continuing if there is insufficient oxygen? .... **(1 mark)**

b) What problems would the creation of lactic acid pose for the body if levels of production were sustained? **(3 marks)**

3 What is the formula for calculating the respiratory quotient for an organism? **(1 mark)**

4 Which organelle of the cell is the site of respiration? .... **(1 mark)**

5 a) What is meant by the term metabolic rate? **(2 marks)**

b) Give three examples of activities that would increase the metabolic rate of an organism. **(3 marks)**

6

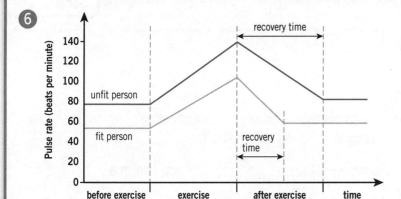

a) What do you notice about the pulse rate of an unfit person in comparison to a fit person during exercise? Explain why this is true. **(2 marks)**

b) What do you notice about the recovery time of the two individuals? Explain why. **(2 marks)**

Score   / 21

How well did you do?

| 0–8 | Try again | 9–16 | Getting there | 17–25 | Good work | 26–34 | Excellent! |

For more information on this topic, see pages 16–17 of your Success Revision Guide.

Biology

Sampling Organisms

Multiple-choice questions

Choose just one answer: A, B, C or D.

1 Which word describes how estimates of population size could be obtained? **(1 mark)**
   A capturing
   B rationing
   C sampling
   D recapturing

2 What rectangular device is used to mark areas for observation? **(1 mark)**
   A quadrat
   B cuboid
   C box
   D transect

3 All the individuals of one species, in a particular area at a particular time are a **(1 mark)**
   A community
   B population
   C habitat
   D ecosystem

4 Which of these is unlikely to be used to capture a flying insect? **(1 mark)**
   A sticky paper
   B pitfall trap
   C UV light trap
   D net

5 Which of these describes a line of quadrats through a habitat? **(1 mark)**
   A transect
   B transport
   C transition
   D transistor

Score   / 5

Short-answer questions

1 Fill in the missing words in the paragraph. (9 marks)

**captivity   habitat   organisms   quadrat   information
number   sample   pooters   pitfall**

Scientists are interested in making links between the .... that live in a

.... and the physical features of the habitat. This .... can be used to

help sustain populations of rare organisms in .... or to provide an understanding of

the impact of human activity on the environment. It is not practical to count the ....

of organisms in a population but instead an estimate based on a .... is used.

Sampling plants can be done by measuring percentage cover or number of individuals in a

.... placed randomly in an area. Samples of animals can be taken using

.... and .... traps.

2 Give an example of a factor which might change and cause zonation along a seashore belt transect. (1 mark)

....

Score   / 10

Answer all parts of all questions. Continue on a separate sheet of paper if necessary.

1 Some students have conducted a survey of their school garden. Use their notes to answer the questions that follow.

> We went out in the garden in our science lesson today. The weather was nice. We searched the whole garden and collected 10 snails. We put a blob of coloured paint on their shell and let them go again. The next day we went back and found 20 snails. Only 2 of the snails we found this time had paint on them. I didn't enjoy the lesson so much because the garden was wet. While we were in the garden we saw a trail of ants leading into a piece of dead wood. We could hear a woodpecker in the neighbouring garden but we didn't see it.

a) Give an example of a habitat mentioned in the notes. .... **(1 mark)**

b) Animal population size can be estimated by the capture-recapture technique. Use this formula to estimate how many snails there are living in the garden. **(2 marks)**

$$\text{Population size} = \frac{\text{number in 1st sample} \times \text{number in 2nd sample}}{\text{number in 2nd sample previously marked}}$$

Show your working.

c) Give one reason why the estimate may be higher than the actual number of snails in the garden. **(1 mark)**

d) Give one other reason why the estimate may be different from the actual number of snails in the garden. **(1 mark)**

e) If the students wanted to estimate the number of ants in the garden, why isn't capture–recapture a practical way of doing this? **(1 mark)**

2 a) What is meant by the term 'artificial ecosystem'? **(1 mark)**

b) Why might an 'artificial' ecosystem have less biodiversity than a 'natural' ecosystem? **(1 mark)**

Score   / 8

How well did you do?

| 1–6 | Try again | 7–12 | Getting there | 13–18 | Good work | 19–23 | Excellent! |

For more information on this topic, see pages 18–19 of your Success Revision Guide.

Biology

Photosynthesis

Multiple-choice questions

Choose just one answer: A, B, C, or D.

1 Which is the energy source for photosynthesis? **(1 mark)**
- **A** chemical
- **B** electrical
- **C** light
- **D** sound

2 Which of these is a raw material for photosynthesis? **(1 mark)**
- **A** carbon dioxide
- **B** oxygen
- **C** glucose
- **D** chemical energy

3 Which of these is NOT required for plant growth? **(1 mark)**
- **A** oxygen
- **B** carbon dioxide
- **C** minerals
- **D** soil

4 Which of these is NOT a rate limiting factor for photosynthesis? **(1 mark)**
- **A** light level
- **B** amount of carbon dioxide
- **C** temperature
- **D** amount of glucose

5 What is the name of the tissue in plant leaves responsible for the majority of photosynthesis? **(1 mark)**
- **A** spongy mesophyll layer
- **B** palisade layer
- **C** xylem
- **D** phloem

Score   / 5

Short-answer questions

1 Which structure in the plant cell is the site of photosynthesis? (1 mark)

2 Lack of magnesium in a plant results in stunted growth and yellow colouring of the plant. What pigment, vital in photosynthesis, is made using magnesium? (1 mark)

3 **True or false?**   True   False   (4 marks)

a) Increasing the temperature from 10°C to 20°C should nearly double the rate of photosynthesis.   ☐   ☐

b) Increasing the temperature from 40°C to 50°C should nearly double the rate of photosynthesis.   ☐   ☐

c) Adding more carbon dioxide will continually increase the amount of photosynthesis the plant can do.   ☐   ☐

d) Increasing the amount of light generally increases the rate of photosynthesis.   ☐   ☐

Score   / 6

Answer all parts of all questions. Continue on a separate sheet of paper if necessary.

1 Examine the diagram of the cross section through a leaf.

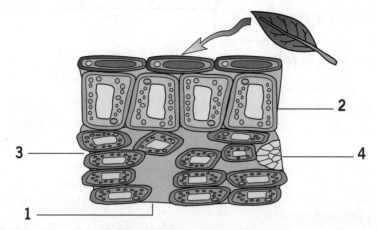

a) Identify the areas labelled **2–4** on the diagram and write them in the table below. **(3 marks)**

b) Describe the roles of these parts of leaf. **(3 marks)**

Number	Name	Role
	leaf vein (containing xylem and phloem)	
	palisade layer	
	spongy mesophyll layer	
1	underside of the leaf	Allows gases and water vapour to enter/ leave the leaf through small pores called stomata.

2 Sodium hydrogencarbonate indicator can be used to give an indication of the amount of carbon dioxide in a solution due to its change in colour at different pHs. The indicator changes in the following ways:

High levels of CO_2 = yellow	Atmospheric levels = red	Low levels of CO_2 = purple

In the following experimental conditions, what would you expect the colour of the indicator to be after 12 hours? Explain your reasons. (Answer on a separate sheet of paper.) **(3 marks)**

a) Open test tube containing indicator and pond water only.

b) Sealed test tube containing indicator, pond water and pond weed only, stored in a well-lit area.

c) Sealed test tube containing indicator, pond water and pond weed only, but covered in tin foil to prevent light entering.

Score   / 9

Biology

How well did you do?

| 0–5 | Try again | 6–10 | Getting there | 11–15 | Good work | 16–20 | Excellent! |

For more information on this topic, see pages 20–21 of your Success Revision Guide.

21

Food Production

Multiple-choice questions

Choose just one answer: A, B, C, or D.

1 Which of these is not easily used by plants to increase biomass? **(1 mark)**
- **A** nitrates
- **B** phosphates
- **C** nitrogen
- **D** magnesium

2 Which of these is the name given to artificial sources of phosphates, nitrates, etc. added to soil? **(1 mark)**
- **A** silage
- **B** manure
- **C** compost
- **D** fertiliser

3 What is the purpose of adding fertiliser to the soil? **(1 mark)**
- **A** increase yield
- **B** increase pests
- **C** decrease yield
- **D** decrease pests

4 Which of these is NOT an allowable organic farming method? **(1 mark)**
- **A** adding artificial fertiliser
- **B** weeding crops
- **C** crop rotation
- **D** using biological control of pests

5 Which of these uses knowledge of osmosis to preserve food? **(1 mark)**
- **A** canning
- **B** salting
- **C** cooking
- **D** freezing

Score / 5

Short-answer questions

1 In each case, identify if the feature is related to intensive farming or organic farming. **(7 marks)**

Feature	Intensive? (✓)	Organic? (✓)
Few hedgerows		
Strips of land maintained 'unfarmed' to allow increased species diversity and encourage natural predators of pests to crops		
Biological control of pests		
Crop rotation including use of nitrogen-fixing crops		
Use of pesticides to reduce the number of weeds and increase crop yield		
Will use a higher amount of genetically modified crops to increase crop resistance to disease or pests for example		
Avoiding planting crops at times when the natural pests are active		

Score / 7

Answer all parts of all questions. Continue on a separate sheet of paper if necessary.

1 Give the reasons why farmers might employ these methods:

a) using pesticides (1 mark)

....

b) using herbicides (1 mark)

....

c) vaccinating their livestock (1 mark)

....

....

d) keeping animals in confined areas (1 mark)

....

....

e) removing hedgerows .... (1 mark)

....

2 Explain how the following methods of food preservation reduce decay by bacteria. (4 marks)

Method	How it works
freezing	
cooking	
adding vinegar	
adding salt	

3 Irradiating food involves exposing it to high levels of radiation, which serves to cause fatal mutations in bacteria. This helps preserve the food. Can foods treated this way be labelled as

organic in the EU? .... (1 mark)

4 Give one use for potassium in plants. (1 mark)

....

5 Give one use for phosphates in plants. (1 mark)

....

Score   / 12

Biology

How well did you do?

| 0–6 | Try again | 7–12 | Getting there | 13–18 | Good work | 19–24 | Excellent! |

For more information on this topic, see pages 22–23 of your Success Revision Guide.

Transport in Animals

Multiple-choice questions

Choose just one answer: A, B, C or D.

1 Which vessels carry blood away
from the heart? **(1 mark)**
 A arteries
 B veins
 C capillaries
 D lymph nodes

2 Which is the liquid part of the blood? **(1 mark)**
 A red blood cells
 B white blood cells
 C platelets
 D plasma

3 Which protein, used for carrying
oxygen, is found in red blood cells? **(1 mark)**
 A haemoglobin
 B immunoglobin
 C fibrin
 D albumin

4 Which vessels carry blood at the
highest pressure? **(1 mark)**
 A arteries
 B veins
 C capillaries
 D lymph nodes

5 Which of these vessels carries blood
from the heart to the lungs? **(1 mark)**
 A vena cava
 B pulmonary vein
 C pulmonary artery
 D aorta

Score / 5

Short-answer questions

1 a) Add name labels to the four chambers of the heart and its four main blood vessels. (8 marks)

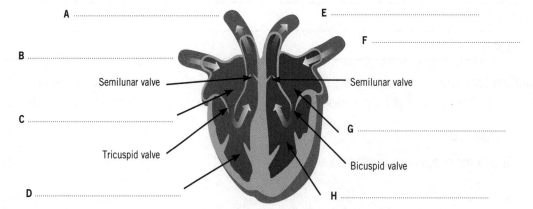

A ....
B ....
C ....
D ....
E ....
F ....
G ....
H ....

Semilunar valve
Semilunar valve
Tricuspid valve
Bicuspid valve

b) Why is the right side of the heart thinner walled than the left side? (2 marks)

....

....

c) What colour is deoxygenated blood? (1 mark)

....

....

Score / 11

Answer all parts of all questions. Continue on a separate sheet of paper if necessary.

 What molecule is formed inside the red blood cell when it is carrying oxygen? **(1 mark)**

....

2

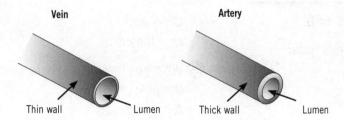

Vein   Artery

Thin wall   Lumen   Thick wall   Lumen

a) Identify a difference shown in the diagrams of the blood vessels above. **(1 mark)**

....

b) Explain why it is necessary for these vessels to differ in this way. **(2 marks)**

....

....

c) Give details of a further difference and its purpose. **(2 marks)**

....

....

....

3 a) In the table below, list three features of red blood cell physiology which make it good at carrying oxygen. **(3 marks)**

b) For each of your answers to **a)**, explain how they benefit the red blood cell in its role. **(3 marks)**

a) Feature	b) Benefit in the role of carrying oxygen

Score   / 12

How well did you do?

| 0–7 | Try again | 8–14 | Getting there | 15–21 | Good work | 20–28 | Excellent! |

For more information on this topic, see pages 24–25 of your Success Revision Guide.

25

Biology

Transport in Plants

Multiple-choice questions

Choose just one answer: A, B, C or D.

1 Which of these vessels carries water around the plant? **(1 mark)**
- **A** artery
- **B** vein
- **C** xylem
- **D** phloem

2 What is the movement of sugars around the plant known as? **(1 mark)**
- **A** transportation
- **B** transpiration
- **C** translocation
- **D** sugar rush

3 What is made up of a tube of dead cells? **(1 mark)**
- **A** artery
- **B** vein
- **C** xylem
- **D** phloem

4 Which of these is likely to be carried in the phloem? **(1 mark)**
- **A** phosphate
- **B** nitrate
- **C** water
- **D** sucrose

5 What name is given to the pull of water through the plant? **(1 mark)**
- **A** transportation
- **B** transpiration
- **C** translocation
- **D** osmosis

Score / 5

Short-answer questions

1 **a)** Where does the water enter the plant? .... (1 mark)

b) By what process does this happen? .... (1 mark)

c) What is it about the cell that makes it particularly well suited to this purpose? (2 marks)

2 **a)** Why are most stomata found on the underside of the leaf? (1 mark)

b) What other features assist with this function? (2 marks)

3 Other than to pull further water up to the leaves for photosynthesis, what purpose does evaporation at the leaves serve for the plant? (1 mark)

Score / 8

Answer all parts of all questions. Continue on a separate sheet of paper if necessary.

1 ✎ When cut flowers are transported, air is introduced into the xylem vessels during periods when the flowers are out of water. This air breaks the transpiration stream. Explain why cutting the bottom off the stalks may prolong the life of the flowers once placed in a vase of water. **(6 marks)**

....

....

....

....

2 a) List four factors that affect the rate of transpiration. **(4 marks)**

....

....

b) For the answers above, explain how the transpiration rate is affected by the factor and the mechanism by which this happens. **(8 marks)**

....

....

....

....

....

c) Which would slow the transpiration rate down more: adding Vaseline to the upper surface or to the lower surface of the leaves? **(1 mark)**

....

d) Explain your answer. **(1 mark)**

....

Score   / 20

How well did you do?

| 0–8 | Try again | 9–16 | Getting there | 17–25 | Good work | 26–33 | Excellent! |

For more information on this topic, see pages 26–27 of your Success Revision Guide.

Digestion and Absorption

Multiple-choice questions

Choose just one answer: A, B, C or D.

1 Which biological molecules are involved in digestion? **(1 mark)**
   A red blood cells
   B white blood cells
   C enzymes
   D lipids

2 Which pH most closely reflects the pH of the stomach? **(1 mark)**
   A pH 2
   B pH 5
   C pH 7
   D pH 10

3 Which of these enzymes is likely to work best in the stomach? **(1 mark)**
   A protease
   B intestinal amylase
   C salivary amylase
   D lipase

4 Which of these is most involved in the physical digestion of food? **(1 mark)**
   A enzymes
   B acid
   C teeth
   D peristalsis

5 What chemical is present in stomach juices which aids digestion? **(1 mark)**
   A mucus
   B hydrochloric acid
   C sulfuric acid
   D sodium hydroxide

Score   / 5

Short-answer questions

1 Give two roles that bile plays in digestion. .... **(2 marks)**

....

....

2 Match the structures of the digestive system with their corresponding functions. **(6 marks)**

Structure	Function
stomach	continues digestion and site of absorption of food
anus	teeth chew food; saliva begins starch digestion
oesophagus	begins protein digestion and kills bacteria on food
mouth	delivers food to the stomach
large intestine	absorption of water
small intestine	food leaves the gut here

Score   / 8

Answer all parts of all questions. Continue on a separate sheet of paper if necessary.

1 What is the benefit of emulsifying fats in terms of lipase action? (1 mark)

2 **a)** What smaller molecules is starch digested into? (1 mark)

b) Why is digestion of food necessary? (2 marks)

3 Describe two features of the small intestine which increase the level of absorption of food. (2 marks)

4 By what process does food enter the blood stream? (1 mark)

5 Into what type of blood vessel would food move from the small intestine? (1 mark)

6 **a)** Food entering the blood system at the small intestine is destined for which organ?

(1 mark)

b) In which blood vessel will it travel to get there? (1 mark)

c) What waste product, produced from the excess protein, is released into the

blood stream? (1 mark)

7 Put these parts of the digestive system in the order they are met by food passing
through them. (6 marks)

oesophagus   mouth   small intestine
anus   stomach   large intestine

Score   / 17

Biology

How well did you do?

0–7 Try again   8–15 Getting there   16–22 Good work   23–30 Excellent!

For more information on this topic, see pages 28–29 of your Success Revision Guide.

Distance, Speed and Velocity

Multiple-choice questions

Choose just one answer: A, B, C or D.

1 The distance moved per unit of
time is the: **(1 mark)**
- **A** velocity
- **B** speed
- **C** magnitude
- **D** displacement

2 What measure is given by the average
speed multiplied by the time taken? **(1 mark)**
- **A** velocity
- **B** acceleration
- **C** distance
- **D** vector

3 What is meant by velocity? **(1 mark)**
- **A** the speed travelled
- **B** the speed over a certain distance
- **C** the speed in a given direction
- **D** the distance travelled in a certain time

4 Vectors have: **(1 mark)**
- **A** magnitude and direction
- **B** direction and speed
- **C** magnitude and speed
- **D** magnitude and distance

5 Which of the following formulae
is correct? **(1 mark)**
- **A** $velocity = \dfrac{speed}{time}$
- **B** $speed = \dfrac{displacement}{time}$
- **C** $velocity = \dfrac{displacement}{time}$
- **D** $velocity = displacement \times time$

Score   / 5

Short-answer questions

1 Calculate the speed of a man who runs 200 m in 40 s. (1 mark)

2 Graphs **A–D** show how your displacement from home (*y*-axis) varies with time (*x*-axis).
Match each graph with the appropriate description from the list below. (4 marks)

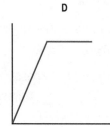

1. You leave home by car to visit a friend. ....

2. You walk to the bus-stop and wait for a bus, which takes you on your journey. ....

3. You move away from home on foot. ....

4. You return home by car. ....

Score   / 5

Answer all parts of all questions. Continue on a separate sheet of paper if necessary.

1 The speed of sound in air is 330 m/s.
Calculate how far away a thunderstorm is, if the thunderclap is heard 4 s after the
lightning flash. (You can assume that the flash is seen instantaneously.) **(2 marks)**

....

....

2 a) Calculate the average speed of a runner who runs a lap of 400 m around a racing
track in 50 s. **(2 marks)**

....

....

b) State the runner's average velocity for the one lap and explain your answer. **(2 marks)**

....

....

3 A boy walks at a speed of 3 m/s for 1 minute. He stops to chat to his friend for 2 minutes.
He then continues, reaching his destination 500 m away from his original starting position in
another 3 minutes.

a) Calculate the distance from the point where
the boy started his journey to the point
where he met his friend. **(2 marks)**

....

b) On the grid alongside, draw a displacement–time
graph for the whole journey. **(4 marks)**

c) At what speed does the boy travel at after
speaking to his friend? **(2 marks)**

....

....

d) What is the average velocity for the whole
journey? **(2 marks)**

....

....

Score   / 16

How well did you do?

| 0–6 | Try again | 7–12 | Getting there | 13–19 | Good work | 20–26 | Excellent! |

For more information on this topic, see pages 32–33 of your Success Revision Guide.

31

Physics

Speed, Velocity and Acceleration

Multiple-choice questions

Choose just one answer: A, B, C or D.

1 What is a change in velocity called? **(1 mark)**
 A speed
 B acceleration
 C displacement
 D distance

2 Which change represents the greatest acceleration? **(1 mark)**
 A from 2 m/s to 5 m/s in 0.5 s
 B from 50 m/s to 15 m/s in 1 s
 C from 100 to 200 m/s in 15 s
 D from stationary to 20 m/s in 2 s

3 Which is the correct unit for acceleration? **(1 mark)**
 A m/s
 B m/s^2
 C m^2/s
 D m^2/s^2

4 The gradient of a velocity–time graph tells us the: **(1 mark)**
 A acceleration
 B displacement
 C speed
 D velocity

5 The area under a velocity–time graph tells us the: **(1 mark)**
 A speed
 B displacement
 C velocity
 D acceleration

Score   / 5

Short-answer questions

1 The velocity–time graph alongside represents a journey. Describe the motion of the object at each of the indicated stages.

 (5 marks)

 A ....

 B ....

 C ....

 D ....

 E ....

2 Draw lines to match the features in the left-hand column to the descriptors in the right-hand column.

(4 marks)

Indication of a stationary object	Gradient of velocity–time graph
Acceleration	Area under velocity–time graph
Distance travelled	Gradient of distance–time graph
Velocity	Horizontal line on distance–time graph

Score   / 9

1 A car moving at 20 m/s decelerates to rest in 5 s after the brakes act, when a pedestrian steps into the road. The driver first takes 1 second to react before the brakes act.

a) On the grid alongside draw a velocity–time graph to represent this motion. **(4 marks)**

b) i) Label the part of the graph that represents the 'thinking distance'. **(1 mark)**

   ii) State the thinking distance in metres. **(1 mark)**

c) i) Label the part of the graph that represents the 'braking distance'. **(1 mark)**

   ii) Calculate the total braking distance. **(1 mark)**

d) Calculate the rate of deceleration whilst braking (assume deceleration was constant). **(2 marks)**

e) Describe how the graph would differ if the braking power was greater. **(1 mark)**

2 a) A car emerging from a side road at 4.5 m/s increases its speed to 17.2 m/s 2.5 s later. Calculate the acceleration of the car. Give your answer to 2 significant figures. **(3 marks)**

b) Describe what feature of a velocity–time graph would indicate that the car subsequently maintained its velocity. **(1 mark)**

Score   / 15

Physics

How well did you do?

| 0–8 | Try again | 9–15 | Getting there | 16–21 | Good work | 22–29 | Excellent! |

Forces

Multiple-choice questions

Choose just one answer: A, B, C or D.

1 What can be said about the forces acting on an object falling at a constant velocity? **(1 mark)**
- **A** there are no forces acting
- **B** all the force of gravity is greater than air resistance
- **C** the drag force is the resultant force
- **D** there is no resultant force

2 The force acting on you due to the Earth is called your: **(1 mark)**
- **A** mass
- **B** weight
- **C** reaction force
- **D** gravity

3 Which force acts to resist the motion of one solid surface across another? **(1 mark)**
- **A** thrust
- **B** lift
- **C** friction
- **D** gravity

4 Which of these statements is true for a skydiver the moment her parachute opens? **(1 mark)**
- **A** air resistance > weight
- **B** weight = air resistance
- **C** air resistance < weight
- **D** air resistance > gravity

5 Without a resultant force a moving object will: **(1 mark)**
- **A** decelerate
- **B** be stationary
- **C** continue at a constant velocity
- **D** lose mass

Score / 5

Short-answer questions

1 Complete the following statements about forces.

a) The force on an object due to the Earth's gravitational pull is called its

.... **(1 mark)**

b) The units used to measure force are .... **(1 mark)**

c) Newton's First Law of Motion states that... **(2 marks)**

....

....

2 a) On a separate piece of paper, draw a diagram of an aircraft in level flight at constant speed and label the four principal forces acting on it. **(4 marks)**

b) State which pairs of forces must be equal to each other. **(2 marks)**

c) State what an aeroplane must weigh if it is kept in level flight by a lift force of 10 kN. **(1 mark)**

Score / 11

GCSE-style questions

Answer all parts of all questions. Continue on a separate sheet of paper if necessary.

❶ The Earth's surface gravitational field strength (g) can be taken as 10 N/kg.

    a) State what a man of mass 70 kg must weigh on the Earth's surface.   **(1 mark)**

    b) On the Moon the gravitational field strength is 1.7 N/kg.

        i) What would the same man's mass be on the Moon?   **(1 mark)**

        ii) What would the same man's weight be on the Moon?   **(1 mark)**

❷ The following data were obtained in an experiment where an increasing force was applied to a suspended spring.

Force applied (N)	Length of spring (cm)
0	15.0
1	17.1
2	19.1
3	20.9
4	23.0
5	24.9
6	27.1
7	29.2
8	32.0
9	36.0

    a) On the graph paper above, plot a graph of force applied against length of spring.   **(4 marks)**

    b) Use your graph to give the length of the spring when a force of 3.5 N is applied.   **(1 mark)**

    c) When an object of unknown mass is hung from the spring it extends by 11.5 cm. Calculate the mass of the object.   **(3 marks)**

Score   / 11

How well did you do?

| 0–8 | Try again | 9–14 | Getting there | 15–20 | Good work | 21–27 | Excellent! |

For more information on this topic, see pages 36–37 of your Success Revision Guide.

35

Physics

Acceleration and Momentum

Multiple-choice questions

Choose just one answer: A, B, C or D.

1 Which one of the following is NOT a vector quantity? **(1 mark)**
- **A** force
- **B** speed
- **C** momentum
- **D** acceleration

2 The purpose of an airbag or crumple zone in a car is to increase the time taken for the driver to stop. What is the advantage of this? **(1 mark)**
- **A** it reduces the driver's momentum
- **B** it reduces the driver's energy
- **C** it reduces the force on the driver
- **D** it reduces the energy of the impact

3 Calculate the momentum of a 60 kg person running at 5 m/s. **(1 mark)**
- **A** 12 kgm/s
- **B** 300 kgm/s
- **C** 120 kgm/s
- **D** 300 kgm/s^2

4 What will a resultant force always cause? **(1 mark)**
- **A** a change in direction
- **B** a change in energy
- **C** a change in speed
- **D** a change in velocity

5 A tennis player returns a serve. How does the force on the ball relate to its momentum? **(1 mark)**
- **A** the force is the rate of change of momentum of the ball
- **B** the force is the overall change of momentum multiplied by the time taken to cause the change
- **C** the force is the momentum of the ball as it is hit
- **D** the force is the momentum of the ball leaving the racket divided by the time taken to cause the change

Score   / 5

Short-answer questions

1 A shopping trolley, which is initially stationary on a smooth, horizontal surface, is given a steady push.

a) Ignoring the effects of friction in the trolley wheels, describe what happens to the trolley.   (2 marks)

....

b) Describe the effect of the following changes.

i) Increasing the mass of the trolley.   (1 mark)

....

ii) Increasing the strength of the push.   (1 mark)

....

2 Newton's Second Law refers to the effect of an unbalanced force on an object. Ring the two phrases that could be used to correctly complete the sentence:

The magnitude of the resultant force on an object is equal to the object's...

final velocity / mass x acceleration / momentum x acceleration / rate of change of momentum / mass x change in velocity

(2 marks)

Score   / 6

Answer all parts of all questions. Continue on a separate sheet of paper if necessary.

1 A boy falls from a climbing frame to the ground in 0.7 s.

a) Taking the value of acceleration due to gravity to be 10 m/s^2, calculate his velocity on impact. **(2 marks)**

b) Calculate the momentum of the boy on impact if his mass is 40 kg. **(1 mark)**

c) If the boy takes 0.2 s to come to rest, calculate the average force exerted on his body. **(2 marks)**

d) Explain the advantage to the boy if the climbing frame had been installed over a safety surface that increases the time taken to break his fall to 0.5 s. **(2 marks)**

2 Wearing seatbelts in cars became compulsory for drivers and front seat passengers in 1992.

a) A car of mass 1000 kg and driver of mass 70 kg travelling at 30 m/s collides with a stationary lorry and rapidly comes to rest. The car's crumple zone offers some protection by reducing the rate of deceleration. The vehicle takes 0.1 s to stop. Calculate the average force exerted on the car driver. **(3 marks)**

b) State one other car safety design that reduces the rate of deceleration. **(1 mark)**

c) Describe the evidence you would expect to support the safety benefit of either of the features mentioned that are designed to reduce the rate of change of momentum on the human body. Include in your answer one piece of data that would be usefully collected. **(2 marks)**

Score   / 13

Physics

How well did you do?

| 0–6 | Try again | 7–12 | Getting there | 13–18 | Good work | 19–24 | Excellent! |

For more information on this topic, see pages 38–39 of your Success Revision Guide.

Pairs of Forces: Action and Reaction

Multiple-choice questions

Choose just one answer: A, B, C or D.

❶ When two objects collide, the momentum afterwards: **(1 mark)**
   A is always more than before
   B is always the same as before
   C is always less than before
   D is always zero

❷ What is the 'reaction' to the 'action' of your weight? **(1 mark)**
   A a force pulling the Earth towards you
   B a force from the ground pushing back on you
   C the force you exert on the ground
   D the force of the Earth pulling you down

❸ Two cars of mass 800 kg and 1000 kg have a head-on collision and come to a standstill. Calculate the speed of the second car, given that the first was moving at 10m/s **(1 mark)**

A 10 m/s   B 8 m/s
C 5 m/s   D 0 m/s

❹ Which of the following is always conserved when objects collide or explode? **(1 mark)**
   A kinetic energy   B velocity
   C momentum   D acceleration

❺ An orbiting spacecraft separates into two sections by means of booster rockets. If section A is half the mass of section B, which of the following is true? **(1 mark)**
   A the velocity of section B will double that of section A
   B the acceleration of each will be the same
   C the change in velocity of section A will be double that of section B
   D the acceleration of section B will be double that of section A

Score   / 5

Short-answer questions

❶ Complete the following passage. (10 marks)

If two objects collide, they each have a change in their momentum because of their change in

.... However, their combined momentum before and afterwards is ....,

so we say that momentum is .... During the collision each object experiences a

.... that causes an acceleration. The size of the force depends on how long it is

acting: a large force acting for a .... time and a smaller force acting for a much

.... time can cause the same change in momentum. The forces experienced by each

object are the same .... because the rate of change of momentum is the same for

each. However, they are in .... directions. The forces are called an ....

and .... pair.

Score   / 10

Answer all parts of all questions. Continue on a separate sheet of paper if necessary.

1 The following diagram shows the Earth and the Moon.

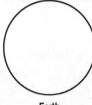

Earth

Moon

a) Using arrows, mark on the diagram the forces experienced by each body due to the gravitational attraction between them. (3 marks)

b) The forces are an action-reaction pair. Describe the relationship between these forces. (2 marks)

c) Below is a diagram showing a person standing on the surface of the Earth.

Indicate the action-reaction pair of forces due to the attraction between the Earth and the person. (3 marks)

2 A 1000 kg car and a 2500 kg truck are travelling at the same speed but in the opposite directions. The vehicles collide head-on.

a) Find an expression for the total momentum of the vehicles before they collide. (3 marks)

b) If the speed each vehicle was initially travelling at was 15 m/s, calculate the velocity of the wreckage immediately after the collision, assuming the two vehicles become entangled and move together as one object. (4 marks)

Score   / 15

How well did you do?

| 0–7 | Try again | 8–15 | Getting there | 16–23 | Good work | 24–30 | Excellent! |

For more information on this topic, see pages 40–41 of your Success Revision Guide.

Physics

Work and Energy

Physics

Multiple-choice questions

Choose just one answer: A, B, C or D.

1 What work is done in lifting a textbook of mass 1.2 kg from the floor to a table at a height of 0.8 m? **(1 mark)**

A 2 J   B 1.5 J
C 9.6 J   D 15 J

2 Which of the following would not affect the work needed to be done against gravity to lift an object? **(1 mark)**

A increasing the mass of the object
B reducing the height difference
C increasing the speed of lifting
D lifting the object on the Moon instead of on the Earth

3 What is the kinetic energy of a 50 kg skateboarder moving at 20 m/s? **(1 mark)**

A 10 kJ   B 1 kJ
C 25 kJ   D 15 kJ

4 A ball of mass 100 g is thrown upwards with a velocity of 10 m/s. What is the maximum height it can reach? **(1 mark)**

A 5 m   B 10 m
C 2.5 m   D 0.5 m

5 An apple falls from a tree and hits the ground 2.5 m below with 3.5 J kinetic energy. What is the mass of the apple? **(1 mark)**

A 8.8 kg   B 140 g
C 350 g   D 1.4 kg

Score   / 5

Short-answer questions

1 A crane raises a load of 500 kg from the ground to the top floor of a construction site at a height of 45 m.

a) Using the value of 10 N/kg for the gravitational field strength, calculate the change in gravitational potential energy (GPE) of the load. **(2 marks)**

b) On the grid alongside, draw a graph to show how the GPE of the load varies with its height during lifting to the top of the building. **(3 marks)**

c) Half-way up, the wire connected to the load snaps.

i) Calculate the kinetic energy of the load when it hits the ground. **(2 marks)**

ii) Calculate the velocity at which the load hits the ground. **(2 marks)**

Score   / 9

Answer all parts of all questions. Continue on a separate sheet of paper if necessary.

1 The diagram shows a rollercoaster ride at a theme park. Initially, the roller coaster is winched mechanically to the starting point (1).

a) 🖋 Explain the motion of the rollercoaster throughout the ride, referring appropriately to gravitational potential energy (GPE) and kinetic energy (KE) transfers at points 2–4. (Answer on a separate sheet) **(6 marks)**

b) Underline the correct answers to complete the following sentence. **(2 marks)**

The maximum height at any point of the ride is determined by **the speed at the lowest point** / **the starting height** / **the total mass** due to conservation of **momentum** / **mass** / **energy**.

c) The combined mass of the rollercoaster and its passengers is 2500 kg.

If the starting height is 40 m, calculate the KE of the roller coaster at point 3, when it is 5 m above the ground. Assume there are no energy losses due to friction. **(3 marks)**

d) Calculate how fast the passengers will be travelling when the rollercoaster passes point 3. **(2 marks)**

e) Without using any further calculations, describe how would your answer to **d)** would differ if an additional 10 passengers with a combined mass of 500 kg had boarded the rollercoaster at the start. **(3 marks)**

Score   / 16

Physics

How well did you do?

| 0–8 | Try again | 9–15 | Getting there | 16–22 | Good work | 23–30 | Excellent! |

For more information on this topic, see pages 42–43 of your Success Revision Guide.

Energy and Power

Multiple-choice questions

Choose just one answer: A, B, C or D.

1 A man does 600 J of work in pushing a child in a toy truck for 15 m. What force does he exert? **(1 mark)**
  - **A** 400 N
  - **B** 40 N
  - **C** 4 N
  - **D** 9000 N

2 Select the correct definition of power. **(1 mark)**
  - **A** power is the amount or work done
  - **B** power is the rate of energy transfer
  - **C** power is the force exerted when doing work
  - **D** power is the maximum energy transfer

3 The Watt, the unit of power, is defined as a: **(1 mark)**
  - **A** J/s
  - **B** Nm
  - **C** kgm/s
  - **D** kgm/s^2

4 Which of the following does not affect thinking distance? **(1 mark)**
  - **A** speed
  - **B** tiredness of the driver
  - **C** condition of the brakes
  - **D** distraction of the driver

5 How much energy is transferred in 6 s at a power of 1.5 kW? **(1 mark)**
  - **A** 4 J
  - **B** 9000 J
  - **C** 250 J
  - **D** 4 kJ

Score   / 5

Short-answer questions

1 A dog weighing 100 N runs up a hill that is 10 m high.

  a) Calculate the dog's energy transfer in working against gravity. (1 mark)

  b) If the dog reaches the top in 4 s, what is the power of the dog? (1 mark)

2 The following graph sketches how the speed of a skydiver changes with time from the moment he leaves the aircraft to just before opening the parachute.

  a) Continue the graph to show how the skydiver's speed changes for the remainder of the descent to Earth. (3 marks)

  b) Select the appropriate words to complete the following sentence. (2 marks)

  At certain stages of the descent the forces acting on the skydiver are **unequal / balanced** so that the acceleration is zero. When this happens the skydiver is said to have reached **final / terminal** velocity.

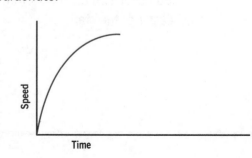

Score   / 7

GCSE-style questions

Answer all parts of all questions. Continue on a separate sheet of paper if necessary.

1 A 31 kg child climbs to the top of a 2.4 m slide and then slides down.

a) Assuming the energy transfer from her gravitational potential energy is 100% efficient, calculate the average rate of kinetic energy transfer if the descent takes 1.2 s. **(3 marks)**

....

....

b) If it took the child 6 s to climb up in the first place, what was the average power of her muscles working against gravity? **(2 marks)**

....

....

2 The driver of a 3 tonne lorry travelling at 80 km/h slams on the brakes when he sees a pedestrian step out into the road 100 m ahead.

a) Calculate the kinetic energy of the lorry. **(2 marks)**

....

b) Calculate the minimum braking force required if the lorry is to stop in time. Give your answer to 2 significant figures. **(2 marks)**

....

c) In the event, the driver actually takes 0.9 s to react.

   i) Calculate the thinking distance. **(2 marks)**

....

   ii) Describe how this affects your answer to part **b)**. **(2 marks)**

....

....

d) Select from the list provided one factor that affects each of the following: **(3 marks)**

   i) thinking distance only ....

   ii) braking distance only ....

   iii) both thinking and braking distance ....

| speed | driver's alertness | road conditions | brake or tyre condition | vehicle load |

Score   / 16

How well did you do?

| 0–7 | Try again | 8–14 | Getting there | 15–21 | Good work | 22–28 | Excellent! |

For more information on this topic, see pages 44–45 of your Success Revision Guide.

Physics

Electrostatic Effects

Multiple-choice questions

Choose just one answer: A, B, C or D.

1 A charged plastic rod is suspended from a thread. A second charged rod, made from a different plastic, is brought near. The suspended rod is attracted to it. What can be concluded? **(1 mark)**
- **A** both rods are negatively charged
- **B** the suspended rod is negatively charged and the second rod is positive
- **C** the two rods have opposite charges
- **D** both rods are positively charged

2 What happens when a Perspex rod is positively charged by rubbing it on a cloth? **(1 mark)**
- **A** positive charges move from the cloth to the rod
- **B** electrons move from the cloth to the rod
- **C** positive and negative charges within the rod become separated at each end
- **D** electrons move from the rod to the cloth

3 A lightening conductor on a tall building works by: **(1 mark)**
- **A** preventing electrostatic charge build-up
- **B** providing a safe route for discharging
- **C** allowing the building to become charged
- **D** insulating the building from the effects of charge in the atmosphere

4 Static charge build-up poses a danger whilst refuelling aircraft. Why? **(1 mark)**
- **A** if the fuel becomes charged it will not burn efficiently in the aircraft engine
- **B** if a charge builds up sufficiently between the aircraft and the tanker there is a risk of discharge, causing an explosion
- **C** it will be more difficult to pump fuel if it has an opposite charge to the tanker
- **D** the charged fuel will charge the aircraft and affect the function of its instruments

Score / 4

Short-answer questions

1 When a balloon is rubbed on a jumper it becomes electrostatically charged. If it is then brought close enough it will be able to attract a small piece of paper, even though this is not charged.

Fill in the missing words to explain how the paper is attracted to the balloon. (5 marks)

.... transfer either from or to the ...., giving it a positive or negative

charge. As the balloon is brought near the paper, the charges on the balloon induce a charge

separation within the piece of paper. The charge on the part of the paper closest to the balloon

is .... to the balloon's charge; these .... charges cause a force

of ....

2 Conductors, such as a piece of metal, cannot be charged by rubbing in this way. What conditions are required to charge a conductor and why? (2 marks)

....

....

....

Score / 7

GCSE-style questions

Answer all parts of all questions. Continue on a separate sheet
of paper if necessary.

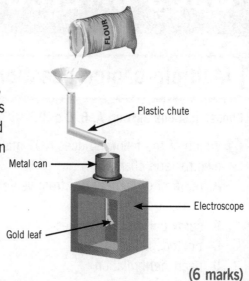

Plastic chute

Metal can

Electroscope

Gold leaf

1 **a)** 🖉 An electroscope is a device that is used to show the
presence of charge. If a charged object is placed on,
or near to, the top plate then the gold leaf rises. This
is because the stem of the electroscope and the gold
leaf then become charged the same and the very thin
gold leaf is repelled.

In the experiment shown, flour is being poured down
a plastic chute into a metal can sitting on top of
an electroscope. Explain how this models the
potential build-up of electrostatic charge in a
flour mill.

(6 marks)

....

....

....

....

....

....

b) A fine dispersion of flour particles in air is readily combustible. Describe how the presence of
electrostatic charge in this environment poses a danger. **(2 marks)**

....

....

c) Explain what measure can be taken to avoid charge building up in the first place. **(2 marks)**

....

....

d) Identify one other situation in which electrostatic charge build-up poses a threat and describe
what is done to minimise the danger in this situation. **(2 marks)**

....

....

Score   / 12

How well did you do?

| 0–6 | Try again | 7–12 | Getting there | 13–18 | Good work | 19–23 | Excellent! |

For more information on this topic, see pages 46–47 of your Success Revision Guide.

Physics

Uses of Electrostatics

Multiple-choice questions

Choose just one answer: A, B, C or D.

1 Which of the following does NOT make use of electrostatic charge? **(1 mark)**
   A removal of particulates from vehicle exhaust gases
   B spray painting car bodies
   C photocopiers
   D heart defibrillation

2 Smoke particles can be removed from chimney exhausts by giving them a charge so that: **(1 mark)**
   A the particles clump together
   B the particles can be trapped on the grid
   C the particles are repelled by the grid
   D the particles can be attracted to the sides of the chimney

3 How do electrostatics aid crop spraying to control pests? **(1 mark)**
   A by ensuring even coverage
   B by activating the insecticide
   C by attracting the insecticide to the pests
   D by positively charging the plants that are sprayed

4 Positively charged paint droplets: **(1 mark)**
   A have gained electrons
   B have gained positive ions
   C have lost electrons
   D have lost positive ions

5 Which of the following is NOT an advantage of spray painting compared to other painting methods? **(1 mark)**
   A paint is used more economically
   B a greater variety of colour is available
   C paint is applied evenly
   D paint droplets repel each other

Score / 5

Short-answer questions

1 Complete the following passage. (7 marks)

A bicycle frame is being prepared for spray painting. The frame is given a positive charge.

The paint spray can is given a .... charge, so that the paint particles are

also given this charge. Because the paint particles all have .... charge they

.... each other to give a finely dispersed spray. The paint particles are

.... by the bicycle frame because it has the .... charge.

This reduces wastage of paint and also ensures that the coverage is ....,

including on parts of the frame facing .... from the spray.

2 A heart defibrillator is charged by connecting it to a power supply.
With reference to charge, describe how this device is used. (3 marks)
(Answer on a separate sheet.)

Score / 10

46

Answer all parts of all questions. Continue on a separate sheet of paper if necessary.

❶ The following diagram shows how a laser printer works.

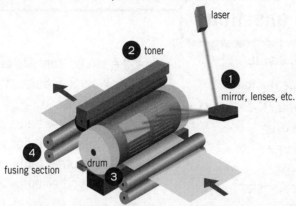

a) The following steps occur when a laser printer is used. Number each statement **1 to 6**, to show the correct sequence. **(5 marks)**

   A light selectively discharges some areas of the drum according to what is to be printed ☐

   B the rotating drum is charged up ☐

   C print toner is attracted to the charged areas only ☐

   D an image of what is to be printed is projected onto the rotating drum using laser light ☐

   E areas that are to be printed black have a different charge to those that will be white ☐

   F the print toner is attracted to the paper and fixed in place by heating ☐

b) What charge would be needed on the paper to help this process if the toner had a negative charge? Explain your answer. **(2 marks)**

....

....

❷ Explain how static charge can be used to remove smoke particles from chimney exhausts. **(4 marks)**

....

....

....

....

....

....

Score   / 11

Physics

How well did you do?

| 0–7 | Try again | 8–14 | Getting there | 15–20 | Good work | 21–26 | Excellent! |

For more information on this topic, see pages 48–49 of your Success Revision Guide.

Electric Circuits

Multiple-choice questions

Choose just one answer: A, B, C or D.

1 Which statement provides the best definition of electric current? **(1 mark)**
- **A** the rate of energy transfer
- **B** the rate of flow of charge
- **C** the flow of electrons
- **D** the amount of charge transfer

2 In a series circuit consisting of a battery and two bulbs, the current: **(1 mark)**
- **A** is highest for the bulb closest to the positive terminal of the battery
- **B** is shared equally between the two components, each having half the total current
- **C** is the same at all points of the circuit
- **D** is zero between the two bulbs

3 A circuit consists of a power pack and six parallel bulbs. What happens if one bulb fails? **(1 mark)**
- **A** the other bulbs all get a lot brighter
- **B** the other bulbs all go out
- **C** the other bulbs all get slightly dimmer
- **D** the other bulbs are unaffected

4 Which one of the following statements about alternating current in a lighting circuit is true? **(1 mark)**
- **A** the direction of charge flow regularly reverses
- **B** positive and negative charge carriers flow alternately
- **C** positive and negative charge carriers flow simultaneously
- **D** periods of charge flow alternate with periods without charge flow

Score   / 4

Short-answer questions

1 Circle the correct options to complete the following explanation. (8 marks)

When a source of electrical energy, such as a battery, is connected into a circuit there will be a flow of **charge / gas / chemicals**, provided the circuit is **in series / continuous / parallel**. This flow is referred to as a **current / circuit / voltage**.

In a wire this involves the movement of **electrons / atoms / chemicals** but the flow is conventionally regarded as being from **positive / negative** to **negative / positive**. This flow is measured in units called **volts / amps / ohms**.

The flow at the positive terminus of the battery is **more than / the same as / less than** that at the negative terminus.

2 In a circuit, a 1.5 V battery provides a current of 750 mA to three identical bulbs connected in parallel.
Calculate the current for the following scenarios. (6 marks)

a) One bulb in the circuit fails ....

b) A 3 V battery is used instead ....

c) The bulbs are replaced with others rated as '1.5 V, 0.2 A' ....

Score   / 14

GCSE-style questions

Answer all parts of all questions. Continue on a separate sheet of paper if necessary.

1 The diagram below shows three identical bulbs connected to a 3 V battery.

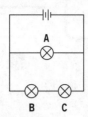

a) Add a switch (labelled X) to the above diagram that will control all three bulbs.   **(1 mark)**

b) Add a second switch (Y) that will control Bulb A only.   **(1 mark)**

c) Explain why it is not possible to use a switch to control Bulbs B and C independently. **(2 marks)**

....

....

d) An ammeter placed adjacent to Bulb A reads 0.2 A. Explain how you can use this information to deduce the reading on an ammeter placed adjacent to the battery (i.e. the total current supplied by the battery). Include the correct reading in your answer.   **(4 marks)**

....

....

....

e) Draw another circuit, using the same components, in which all three bulbs have equivalent voltage and current readings to Bulb A.   **(2 marks)**

f) Calculate the total current when a fourth equivalent bulb is added to your new circuit in parallel.   **(2 marks)**

....

....

Score   / 12

How well did you do?

| 0–8 | Try again | 9–14 | Getting there | 15–22 | Good work | 23–30 | Excellent! |

For more information on this topic, see pages 50–51 of your Success Revision Guide.

Voltage or Potential Difference

Physics

Multiple-choice questions

Choose just one answer: A, B, C or D.

1 What does a voltmeter measure? **(1 mark)**
  - **A** the flow of electricity
  - **B** the electrical power
  - **C** the electrical energy transfer in a component
  - **D** the energy transfer per unit charge

2 Which unit is used for charge? **(1 mark)**
  - **A** amp   **B** coulomb
  - **C** joule   **D** volt

3 How should an ammeter and a voltmeter be connected in a circuit? **(1 mark)**
  - **A** both are connected in parallel
  - **B** both are connected in series
  - **C** the ammeter is connected in series; the voltmeter is connected in parallel
  - **D** the voltmeter is connected in series; the ammeter is connected in parallel

4 What voltage is required to give 0.5 C of charge 4.5 J of energy? **(1 mark)**
  - **A** 9 V
  - **B** 5 V
  - **C** 2.25 V
  - **D** 0.11 V

5 Which statement is NOT true for a series circuit consisting of a 1.5 V cell, a switch and two identical bulbs? **(1 mark)**
  - **A** with the switch closed, each bulb has a potential difference of 0.75 V
  - **B** with the switch open, each bulb has a potential difference of 1.5 V
  - **C** with the switch closed, the current is the same through each bulb
  - **D** with the switch open, neither bulb is on because no current flows

Score / 5

Short-answer questions

1 True or false?   True   False   **(6 marks)**
  - **a)** non-identical bulbs connected in series have the same current   ☐   ☐
  - **b)** identical bulbs connected in parallel have the same current   ☐   ☐
  - **c)** non-identical bulbs connected in series have the same potential difference   ☐   ☐
  - **d)** non-identical bulbs connected in parallel have the same potential difference   ☐   ☐
  - **e)** identical bulbs connected in series have the same potential difference   ☐   ☐
  - **f)** non-identical bulbs connected in parallel have the same current   ☐   ☐

2 For the circuit alongside, calculate the readings on the given ammeters and voltmeters. The bulbs are all identical.

  (4 marks)

  a) A_3 ....

  b) A_4 ....

  c) V_2 ....

  d) V_3 ....

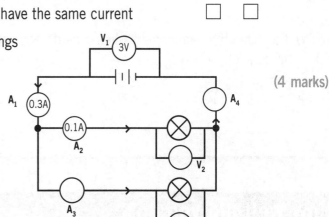

Score / 10

50

Answer all parts of all questions. Continue on a separate sheet of paper if necessary.

1 Twenty-five students were asked to build a circuit from the following components:
- two identical bulbs
- one 3 V battery
- voltmeters to measure the potential difference across each bulb

a) On a separate piece of paper, draw each of the different types of circuit that the students could have built. Take care to use the correct symbols. **(4 marks)**

b) How does the brightness of the bulbs in each circuit compare? Explain your answer. **(3 marks)**

c) The results obtained by the students are grouped in the table below:

Group	Number of students	Bulb X	Bulb Y
A	14	1.5 V	1.5 V
B	10	3.0 V	3.0 V
C	1	1.5 V	3.0 V

i) What might explain the results obtained by the student in Group C? **(2 marks)**

ii) Suggest how you could test your answer to part **i)** **(1 mark)**

d) State the type of circuit built by each of the following groups: **(2 marks)**

i) Group A:

ii) Group B:

e) Calculate the current in the circuit built by Group A, if the energy transfer in each bulb is 0.3 J every second. **(3 marks)**

Score   / 15

How well did you do?

| 0–8 | Try again | 9–14 | Getting there | 15–22 | Good work | 23–30 | Excellent! |

For more information on this topic, see pages 52–53 of your Success Revision Guide.

51

Physics

Resistance and Resistors

Multiple-choice questions

Choose just one answer: A, B, C or D.

1 Resistance in a metal is due to: **(1 mark)**
   - **A** collisions of electrons with the lattice ions
   - **B** restricted movement of the lattice ions
   - **C** the voltage applied
   - **D** freely moving electrons

2 A component whose resistance has a fixed value for a range of potential differences is said to obey which law? **(1 mark)**
   - **A** Coulomb's Law
   - **B** Newton's Law
   - **C** Ohm's Law
   - **D** the law of conservation of energy

3 Which of the following is NOT true for a fixed resistor? **(1 mark)**
   - **A** doubling the voltage doubles the current
   - **B** the combined resistance of two parallel resistors is half that of one alone
   - **C** putting two such resistors in series has no effect on the current for a given voltage
   - **D** halving the current halves the voltage

4 What is the combined resistance of three 10 Ω resistors in series? **(1 mark)**
   - **A** 1000 Ω
   - **B** 30 Ω
   - **C** 3.3 Ω
   - **D** 10 Ω

5 Resistors X and Y are connected in series to a 3 V battery. A current of 0.2 A flows through resistor X. A potential difference of 2 V is measured for resistor Y. What are the values of X and Y? **(1 mark)**
   - **A** X=10 Ω; Y=5 Ω
   - **B** X=15 Ω; Y=5 Ω
   - **C** X=6 Ω; Y=12 Ω
   - **D** X=5 Ω; Y=10 Ω

Score / 5

Short-answer questions

1 Metals are thought of as a lattice of stationary positive ions surrounded by free electrons.

   a) State which feature of this structure explains the electrical conductivity of metals. (1 mark)

   b) Describe what happens if a potential difference is applied across the piece of metal. (1 mark)

   c) What is different about the structure and behaviour of an insulator compared to metals? (1 mark)

2 A fixed resistance of 10 Ω is connected to a 3 V battery.

   a) Calculate the current that flows. (1 mark)

   b) What would be the effect of adding a second, identical resistor in series? (1 mark)

   c) What would be the effect of adding a second, identical resistor in parallel? (1 mark)

Score / 6

Answer all parts of all questions. Continue on a separate sheet of paper if necessary.

1 Resistance can be thought of as a 'force' opposing a current.

a) State which feature of the structure of metals causes resistance? **(1 mark)**

....

b) The potential difference across a resistor indicates the difference in energy per unit charge flowing into and out of the resistor. Explain what accounts for this energy difference. **(2 marks)**

....

....

c) Describe how resistance is defined. Remember to state the unit used. **(2 marks)**

....

....

2 A bulb with resistance 8 Ω is connected in series with a second bulb of 16 Ω. Both bulbs are then connected to a 3 V battery.

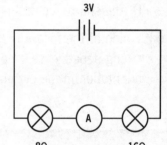

a) Calculate the reading on an ammeter placed between the bulbs. **(1 mark)**

....

b) Calculate the potential difference across each of the bulbs. **(2 marks)**

....

....

c) i) What would be the current through each bulb if they were connected in parallel to the battery? **(2 marks)**

....

....

ii) Use your answer to part **i)** to calculate the total current from the battery and, therefore, the effective resistance of the two bulbs together. **(2 marks)**

....

....

....

Score   / 12

How well did you do?

| 0–6 | Try again | 7–12 | Getting there | 13–18 | Good work | 19–23 | Excellent! |

For more information on this topic, see pages 54–55 of your Success Revision Guide.

Physics

Special Resistors

Multiple-choice questions

Choose just one answer: A, B, C or D.

❶ Which of the following resistors could be used to control a thermostat? **(1 mark)**
- **A** light-dependent resistor
- **B** diode
- **C** thermistor
- **D** light-emitting diode

❷ Which of the following does not make use of a variable resistor? **(1 mark)**
- **A** the volume control on a radio
- **B** a dimmer switch for a light
- **C** the 'charging' light on a rechargeable device
- **D** the shutter control on a camera

❸ Which of the following components shows a strong dependence on polarity (i.e. its orientation in the circuit)? **(1 mark)**
- **A** diode
- **B** thermistor
- **C** LDR
- **D** variable resistor

❹ The initials NTC are applied to a component called a thermistor. What do the initials stand for? **(1 mark)**
- **A** non-thermal conductor
- **B** negative terminal charge
- **C** negative temperature coefficient
- **D** new thermal component

❺ A variable resistor was used to set the current in a circuit to 0.3 A. What resistance did it have if its p.d. was 1.5 V? **(1 mark)**
- **A** 0.45 Ω
- **B** 0.2 Ω
- **C** 5 Ω
- **D** 1.5 Ω

Score / 5

Short-answer questions

❶ During its operation a filament bulb gets hot.

a) Explain how temperature affects resistance in this case. (2 marks)

b) Describe how your answer to part **a)** differs from the behaviour of a thermistor. (1 mark)

c) The grid below displays a graph of the dependence of current on voltage for a thermistor. Add a second graph showing what you would expect if you were to do the same experiment at a higher temperature. (1 mark)

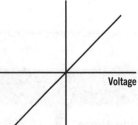

Score / 4

Physics

Answer all parts of all questions. Continue on a separate sheet of paper if necessary.

1 The following graph shows how the current through a filament bulb varies with applied voltage.

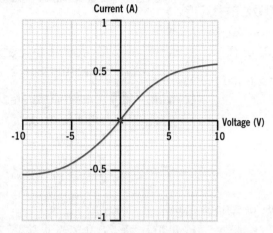

a) Calculate the resistance of the bulb for the given applied voltages: **(2 marks)**

   i) 2 V ....

   ii) 6 V ....

b) Would you describe the bulb as an Ohmic or non-Ohmic conductor? Explain your answer. **(2 marks)**

   ....

   ....

c) On the axes below, sketch the graph you might expect if you were to carry out the same
   experiment using a diode instead of the bulb. **(3 marks)**

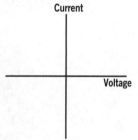

d) Describe the role of a diode in a circuit. **(1 mark)**

   ....

2 Describe the resistance behaviour shown by a component known as a 'LDR'. **(2 marks)**

   ....

   ....

   ....

Score   / 10

How well did you do?

| 0–5 | Try again | 6–10 | Getting there | 11–15 | Good work | 16–19 | Excellent! |

For more information on this topic, see pages 56–57 of your Success Revision Guide.

55

Physics

The Mains Supply

Multiple-choice questions

Choose just one answer: A, B, C or D.

1 What colour is the live wire in the mains
electricity supply? **(1 mark)**
- **A** red
- **B** blue
- **C** brown
- **D** green and yellow

2 Which of the following best describes mains
electricity? **(1 mark)**
- **A** 230 Hz a.c., 50 V
- **B** 50 Hz a.c., 230 V
- **C** 100 Hz a.c., 230 V
- **D** 60 Hz a.c., 115 V

3 Which of the following is NOT a safety feature
for use with mains electricity? **(1 mark)**
- **A** RCCB
- **B** use of alternating current
- **C** double insulation
- **D** earthing

4 A mains-operated television requires 0.25 A.
What is its approximate power rating? **(1 mark)**
- **A** 60 W
- **B** 1k W
- **C** 1m W
- **D** 15 W

5 A device is rated at using 4.2 A. What fuse
rating is most appropriate? **(1 mark)**
- **A** 5 A
- **B** 3 A
- **C** 13 A
- **D** 1 A

Score   / 5

Short-answer questions

1 The diagram shows the
inside of a mains plug.

a) Add labels for the
indicated parts of a
mains plug. **(5 marks)**

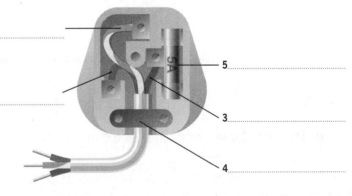

1..............................

2..............................

5..............................

3..............................

4..............................

b) Explain the function of component 5 and how it works. **(2 marks)**

....

....

c) The maximum current rating of a mains-operated device is 13 A. Calculate the maximum power
of such a device, giving the answer to 2 significant figures in kW. **(2 marks)**

....

....

Score   / 9

Answer all parts of all questions. Continue on a separate sheet of paper if necessary.

1 A key safety feature of the mains electricity supply is the inclusion of an earth wire. A device that has an external case made entirely of plastic, such as a hair-drier, does not need an earth connection.

a) Explain what it means to 'earth' something, indicating how this protects the user of the equipment in the event of an electrical fault. **(3 marks)**

b) Describe why a device with an external case made entirely of plastic, does not need an earth connection. You should include the correct term for this type of protection in your answer. **(2 marks)**

2 The picture opposite shows a residual current circuit breaker (RCCB) that is recommended for use with power tools. The RCCB plugs into the socket before the power tool is plugged into the RCCB.

a) Describe what is meant by 'residual current'?

(1 mark)

b) Describe how the RCCB offers protection to the person using the power tool. **(2 marks)**

c) Explain why using a circuit breaker is better than relying on just the fuse. **(2 marks)**

Score   / 10

How well did you do?

| 0–6 | Try again | 7–12 | Getting there | 13–18 | Good work | 19–24 | Excellent! |

For more information on this topic, see pages 58–59 of your Success Revision Guide.

Physics

Atomic Structure

Multiple-choice questions

Choose just one answer: A, B, C or D.

1 Which of the following most accurately
describes atomic structure? **(1 mark)**
 A the atom is made of positively charged
 material with embedded electrons
 B neutrons orbit a nucleus composed of
 protons and electrons
 C electrons orbit a nucleus composed of
 protons and neutrons
 D proton-electron pairs orbit a nucleus
 composed of neutrons

2 In the symbols used to represent an atom, Z
represents the number of: **(1 mark)**
 A protons
 B neutrons
 C charges
 D electrons

3 An isotope of carbon has 6 protons and
6 neutrons. A second isotope has 8 neutrons;
what is its mass number? **(1 mark)**
 A 6 **B** 8
 C 12 **D** 14

4 What are protons and neutrons collectively
known as? **(1 mark)**
 A isotopes
 B ions
 C atoms
 D nucleons

5 During nuclear decay, which of the following
may NOT be conserved? **(1 mark)**
 A charge
 B number of protons
 C atomic mass
 D number of nucleons

Score / 5

Short-answer questions

1 Our modern view of the atom involves particles known as electrons, protons and neutrons.
 a) Complete the following table of properties of these particles. (4 marks)

Particle	Relative mass	Charge
Electron	$\dfrac{1}{1840}$	
Proton		+1
Neutron		

 b) State the relationship between the number of electrons and the number of protons for
 any given neutral atom. (1 mark)

....

2 How many protons, neutrons and electrons do the following have? (3 marks)
 a) neutral atom of $^{56}_{26}Fe$ ....
 b) a neutral atom of $^{32}_{15}P$ ....
 c) a K+ ion of $^{39}_{19}K$ ....

Score / 8

GCSE-style questions

Answer all parts of all questions. Continue on a separate sheet of paper if necessary.

1 As knowledge of atomic structure has developed, scientists have revised the working model of the atom.

a) With the aid of a diagram, describe the model devised by J.J. Thompson, usually referred to as the 'plum pudding' model. **(3 marks)**

b) A classic experiment by Geiger and Marsden led Ernest Rutherford to propose an entirely different model of the atom. The surprising finding was that alpha particles were occasionally deflected or bounced back when fired at a very thin piece of gold foil, though most went straight through. From the following list select two conclusions that Rutherford drew from these observations. Tick the correct statements. **(2 marks)**

A Atomic nuclei contain neutrons. ☐

B Alpha particles are positively charged. ☐

C The mass of the atom is concentrated in a very small region. ☐

D Gold atoms are positively charged. ☐

E Most of the atom is empty space. ☐

2 A text book refers to the following isotopes of oxygen:

$$^{16}_{8}O \quad ^{17}_{7}O \quad ^{17}_{8}O \quad ^{18}_{8}O$$

a) Explain why at least one of these must be incorrect. **(2 marks)**

b) Describe what is meant by the term 'isotope'. **(2 marks)**

3 Some atoms are unstable and undergo radioactive decay. Complete the following alpha decay equation for radon: **(2 marks)**

$$^{222}_{86}Rn \longrightarrow {}^{\square}_{\square}Po + {}^{4}_{2}He$$

Score   / 11

How well did you do?

| 0–6 | Try again | 7–12 | Getting there | 13–18 | Good work | 19–24 | Excellent! |

For more information on this topic, see pages 60–61 of your Success Revision Guide.

Physics

Radioactive Decay

Multiple-choice questions

Choose just one answer: A, B, C or D.

1 What is a beta particle? **(1 mark)**
 A an electron from the atom
 B a helium nucleus
 C a fast moving electron emitted by the nucleus
 D high frequency electromagnetic radiation

2 What is gamma radiation effectively stopped by? **(1 mark)**
 A the outer layer of skin
 B 5 mm thickness of lead
 C several metres of concrete
 D 5 mm thickness of aluminium

3 A radioisotope sample has 8×10^9 undecayed nuclei. How many will remain 1 hour later if the half-life is 15 min? **(1 mark)**
 A 2×10^9
 B 5×10^8

 C 2.5×10^8
 D 1×10^9

4 Carbon-14 is a radioactive isotope, $^{14}_{6}C$. Which of the following represents a Carbon-14 atom following beta decay? **(1 mark)**
 A $^{15}_{6}N$
 B $^{15}_{7}N$
 C $^{13}_{5}N$
 D $^{14}_{7}N$

5 During gamma decay: **(1 mark)**
 A there is no change to the nucleus
 B the nucleus relaxes to a lower energy state
 C nuclear particles disintegrate
 D radio waves are emitted

Score / 5

Short-answer questions

1 True or false? True False **(6 marks)**
 a) All atoms of all elements undergo radioactive decay. ☐ ☐
 b) Alpha particles have the least ability to penetrate matter. ☐ ☐
 c) When atoms undergo gamma decay the element changes. ☐ ☐
 d) Particles released by radioactive decay can cause ionisation of matter. ☐ ☐
 e) A sheet of paper is sufficient to stop alpha particles. ☐ ☐
 f) When atoms decay there is always a reduction in the atomic number. ☐ ☐

2 A sample of a radioisotope is monitored and it is found that there are 4.8×10^5 disintegrations in 2 minutes.
 a) Ring the option below that shows the activity of this sample. **(1 mark)**

   4000 Bq   400 Bq   480 000 Bq   240 000 Bq   8000 Bq

 b) If the half-life of the radioisotope is 2.5 h, calculate the activity expected after 7.5 h. **(2 marks)**

Score / 9

Answers

Abbreviations used

;	separates marking points
ORA	or reverse argument
OWTTE	or words to that effect

For questions marked ✐, where marks are awarded for the quality of written communication, model answers have been provided. The model answers would score the full 6 marks available. If you have made most of the points given in the model answer and communicated your ideas clearly, in a logical sequence with few errors in spelling, punctuation and grammar, you would get 6 marks. You will lose marks if some of the points are missing, if the answer lacks clarity or if there are serious errors in spelling, punctuation and grammar.

Pages 4–5 Cells and Organisation

Multiple-choice questions
1. B 2. C 3. D 4. A 5. B

Short-answer questions
1. a) true b) false c) false d) true
   e) true f) true (but actually much smaller ones too!)
   g) true h) false i) true

GCSE-style questions
1. a) 1 plant; 2 animal
   b) **A** chloroplast; **B** vacuole; **C** mitochondria; **D** cell wall; **E** cell membrane; **F** ribosome; **G** cytoplasm; **H** nucleus; **I** ribosome; **J** cell membrane; **K** cytoplasm; **L** nucleus
   c) mitochondria – site of respiration; chloroplasts – harnesses energy for photosynthesis; cytoplasm – site of many cellular reactions (in solution)
2. an organ; because it contains more than one tissue type. (BUT 'muscle' is a type of tissue because it is made only of muscle cells.)
3. **Any three from:** need to communicate between cells; hard to supply cells with nutrients; hard to remove cell waste; harder to exchange substances with their environment

Pages 6–7 DNA and Protein Synthesis

Multiple-choice questions
1. D 2. B 3. C 4. B 5. A

Short-answer questions
1. a) triplet code (codon) b) one
   c) translation d) a ribosome
   e) in the cytoplasm
   f) DNA is double stranded whereas RNA is single stranded (another difference is that DNA contains the bases ATCG but RNA contains AUCG)
2. a) false b) true c) true

GCSE-style questions
1.

A	B	E	G	C	D	F

2. mRNA is small, double stranded DNA is too big.
3. cell wall (in a plant)
4. spiral
5. sugar (called deoxyribose); and phosphate
6. protein > chromosome > gene > base

Pages 8–9 Proteins and Enzymes

Multiple-choice questions
1. B 2. D 3. B 4. B 5. D

Short-answer questions
1. **Any three from:** respiration; photosynthesis; DNA replication; digestion; protein synthesis; DNA transcription; DNA translation; cutting DNA; resealing DNA (in genetic engineering)
2. structural (e.g. collagen); hormones (e.g. insulin); enzymes (e.g. pepsin); carrier molecules (e.g. haemoglobin)
3. a) to digest (food) stains

   b) enzymes denature; at temperatures above 40°C (although some enzymes are stable at much higher temperatures than this e.g. in volcanic bacteria, this is the general rule for mammalian enzymes)

GCSE-style questions
1. amino acids
2. a) biological = originating in living matter; catalysts = chemicals which speed up reactions
   b) enzymes
3. a) pH = 7.5–8.0 b) small intestine/mouth
   c) denatured
   d) shape of the active site has altered; so that the substrate no longer fits/the lock and key function no longer works
   e) enzymes are specific/one enzyme works on only one type of substrate; each enzyme fits its own substrate perfectly

Pages 10–11 Cell Division

Multiple-choice questions
1. C 2. C 3. C 4. B 5. D

Short-answer questions
1. a) haploid b) gametes (accept egg/sperm)
   c) fertilisation d) sexual reproduction
2. DNA; gene; proteins; variation; mutations; changes; insignificant.

GCSE-style questions
1. a) 46 (23 pairs) b) 23
   c) testes d) meiosis
   e) variation in the offspring
2.

F	D	A	B	E	C

3. Bacteria reproduce by mitosis; so normally there is limited variation in a population; natural mutations may give resistance to anti-bacterial substances; anti-bacterial substances kill some bacteria and leave the resistant ones living to reproduce; thus the population has evolved new strains.

Pages 12–13 Growth and Development

Multiple-choice questions
1. D 2. B 3. D 4. A 5. C

Short-answer questions
1.

gene switching	ability to stop expression of some genes in favour of others
gamete	sex cell e.g. sperm or egg, pollen or ovule
differentiated	specialised for a specific job – not all genes switched on
embryo	fertilised egg in the early stages of development
embryonic stem cell	completely unspecialised cell taken before the eight cell stage of an embryo or found in umbilical cord blood
stem cell	unspecialised cell which has all the genes present in its nucleus switched on

2. All are potential uses so all should be ticked

GCSE-style questions
1. a) Javelle b) Mark/Erica c) Ella
2. a)

B	D	A	E	C	F	G

   Marks awarded: B before D; D before A; A before E; E before C; C before F
   b) wet mass (or fresh biomass)
   c) to ensure all the water has been removed

Pages 14–15 Transport in Cells

Multiple-choice questions
1. B 2. A 3. A 4. A 5. C

Short-answer questions
1.

2. a) diffusion b) diffusion c) diffusion d) osmosis
   e) diffusion

GCSE-style questions
1. A higher concentration of minerals in the soil than in the plant; means that water would move out of the plant cells into the soil; by osmosis; meaning the plants would dehydrate/wilt and possibly die.
2. Inside the cell would be a higher concentration of solutes than outside (ORA); so water moves into the cells; by osmosis; the cell enlarges/swells; (the lack of cell wall means there is nothing to prevent the increased pressure) bursting the cell.
3. a) i) further increase in mass; until the cell is turgid
      ii) More time is available for; more water to move in by osmosis.
   b) about 0.15M (the point where there is no net change in mass)
   c) i) No further loss in mass/the final mass would be about the same.
      ii) The potato cells have lost all their water to the solution already; they are already fully flaccid.

Pages 16–17 Respiration

Multiple-choice questions
1. A 2. C 3. B 4. D 5. D

Short-answer questions
1.

Substance	Product of aerobic respiration	Product of anaerobic respiration
glucose		
carbon dioxide	✓	
lactic acid		✓
energy	✓	✓
water	✓	
oxygen		

2. a) fermentation b) carbon dioxide c) ethanol

GCSE-style questions
1. ✐ During the race, the cells in the athlete's muscles must respire to produce energy. However, oxygen is used at a faster rate than it can be taken into the body. This forces the muscle cells to respire anaerobically for a short time, creating an oxygen debt and a build-up of lactic acid. After the race, the oxygen debt must be repaid so that the lactic acid can be broken down. The athlete continues to breathe heavily after the race so that as much oxygen can be taken on board as possible in a short time. This is called excessive post-exercise oxygen consumption (EPOC).
2. a) cramp
   b) Acidification of the blood/tissue; could result in enzymes being denatured; which would slow metabolism.
3. RQ = volume of carbon dioxide produced ÷ volume of oxygen used
4. mitochondria
5. a) Metabolic rate is a measure of the number of chemical reactions that occur in the body; within a specific amount of time.

Answers

b) **Any three from:** increased synthesis of tissue (growth or repair); increased muscle action; increased need to generate heat (entering a colder area in homeotherms); increased active transport; increased digestion

6. **a)** Pulse is higher in the unfit person than the fit person (ORA); Because the less fit the person is the less oxygen they can transport in the same amount of time. (OWTTE)

   b) The fitter person recovers more quickly (ORA); Because they are able to repay the oxygen debt faster by transporting oxygen round the body more efficiently. (OWTTE)

Pages 18–19 Sampling Organisms

Multiple-choice questions
1. C   2. A   3. B   4. B   5. A
Short-answer questions
1. organisms; habitat; information; captivity; number; sample; quadrat; pooters; pitfall.
2. **Any one from:** salinity; exposure to the air; exposure to the sea; degree to which it is covered by the tides.
GCSE-style questions
1. **a)** dead wood (or garden habitat)
   b) $\frac{10 \times 20}{2}$; = 100
   c) **Any one from:** The paint may have made the snails more visible to predators so more of the painted ones were eaten, meaning that less were recaptured than there should have been; the wet weather may have washed paint off of some of the snails that were recaptured so they may not have correctly been recorded.
   d) **Any one from:** The weather had affected the number of snails out in the garden; the number of individuals in all the samples was quite small; the snails that were captured the first time might be more prone to being captured again and this could influence the results; marking the snails could have injured them so that they did not move and were recaptured the next day.
   e) Ants are too small to mark and recapture.
2. **a)** a man-made habitat and climate
   b) Tight control of the physical and chemical components of the ecosystem would mean there is less variety in the habitat and so less likely to be variety in the biological organisms that inhabit it.

Pages 20–21 Photosynthesis

Multiple-choice questions
1. C   2. A   3. D   4. D   5. B
Short-answer questions
1. chloroplast
2. chlorophyll
3. **a)** true   **b)** false   **c)** false   **d)** true
GCSE-style questions
1. a) and b)

Number	Name	Role
4	Leaf vein (containing xylem and phloem)	**Carries water to the leaf (xylem); and sugars around the plant (phloem)**
3	Palisade layer	**Site of photosynthesis**
2	Spongy mesophyll layer	**Allows exchange of gases (such as carbon dioxide, water vapour and oxygen)**
1	Underside of the leaf	Allows gases and water vapour to enter/leave the leaf through small pores called stomata

2. **a)** red – Atmospheric level of CO_2
   b) purple – Rate of photosynthesis > respiration (growth in the plants leading to CO_2 in the water being used up.
   c) yellow – Plants respiring increases the amount of CO_2 in the water. (Foil prevents photosynthesis).

Pages 22–23 Food Production

Multiple-choice questions
1. C   2. D   3. A   4. A   5. B
Short-answer questions
1.

Feature	Intensive? (✓)	Organic? (✓)
Few hedgerows	✓	
Strips of land maintained 'unfarmed' to allow increased species diversity and encourage natural predators of pests to crops		✓
Biological control of pests		✓
Crop rotation including use of nitrogen-fixing crops		✓
Use of pesticides to reduce the number of weeds and increase crop yield	✓	
Will use a higher amount of genetically modified crops to increase crop resistance to disease or pests for example	✓	
Avoiding planting crops at times when the natural pests are active		✓

GCSE-style questions
1. **a)** to reduce damage to crops by pests
   b) to increase yield of crops by reducing competition
   c) to reduce risk of disease (resulting in contamination of meat, milk, eggs, etc.)
   d) to maximise the conversion of food to biomass (and minimise losses as heat or in movement)
   e) to increase efficiency by allowing large-scale machinery to move around the farm
2.

Method	How it works
freezing	Chemical reactions happen in solution. When frozen, decomposers cannot therefore respire or reproduce.
cooking	Heating denatures the enzymes in bacteria, preventing respiration and other chemical reactions from happening.
adding vinegar	Acidity denatures the enzymes in bacteria, preventing respiration and other chemical reactions from happening.
adding salt	Salting means bacteria lose water by osmosis and then dehydrate, making cellular respiration impossible.

3. no
4. to help enzymes involved in respiration and photosynthesis
5. component of DNA and cell membranes

Pages 24–25 Transport in Animals

Multiple-choice questions
1. A   2. D   3. A   4. A   5. C
Short-answer questions
1. **a)** **A** pulmonary artery; **B** vena cava; **C** right atrium; **D** right ventricle; **E** aorta; **F** pulmonary vein; **G** left atrium; **H** left ventricle
   b) Thinner walled right side produces blood at lower pressure; because it supplies the lungs which are close and delicate.
   c) (dark) red
GCSE-style questions
1. oxyhaemoglobin
2. **a)** **Any one from:** Walls of the artery are thicker than those of the vein (ORA); The lumen is wider in the veins.
   b) **Any two from:** Artery walls (contain larger amounts of elastic) to withstand; and maintain; high blood pressures.
   c) Larger lumen in veins; to avoid restriction to blood flow OR smaller lumen in arteries; to maintain high blood pressure OR valves present in veins; to prevent back flow of blood.

3. a) and b) (1 mark per correct box)

Feature	Benefit in the role of carrying oxygen
biconcave shape	to maximise surface area for diffusion of oxygen
no nucleus	to maximise room for oxygen to be carried
contain haemoglobin	to maximise ability to carry oxygen

Pages 26–27 Transport in Plants

Multiple-choice questions
1. C   2. C   3. C   4. D   5. B
Short-answer questions
1. **a)** roots (root hair cells)
   b) osmosis
   c) large surface area; limited cell contents
2. **a)** to reduce water loss by evaporation (the underside is out of the sun)
   b) waterproof waxy cuticle; ability to close stomata
3. cools the plant
GCSE-style questions
1. 🖉 Air bubbles in the plants stem will prevent effective transpiration, so the plant will not be able to take up water, or photosynthesise. As a result, it will wilt from lack of water and die from lack of food. Cutting the stem may remove the portion of stem containing the air bubbles, so that when the flowers are placed in water, transpiration can take place again, helping to prolong the life of the flowers.
2. **a)** temperature; humidity; light intensity; wind
   b) **temperature** – Increase in temperature increases evaporation; and therefore increases transpiration.
   humidity – Increase in humidity reduces transpiration; since water cannot easily move into the area around the leaf which is already occupied by water molecules.
   light intensity – Increased light intensity increases transpiration; because it opens the stomata, leading to increased water loss by evaporation.
   wind – Increased wind carries water molecules away, maintaining the osmosis gradient and increasing water loss; and hence increasing transpiration rate (**1 mark for the effect on transpiration rate; 1 mark for the process**)
   c) lower surface
   d) There are more stomata on the lower surface.

Pages 28–29 Digestion and Absorption

Multiple-choice questions
1. C   2. A   3. A   4. C   5. B
Short-answer questions
1. emulsifies fats (breaks into droplets); neutralises stomach acid
2.

stomach	begins protein digestion and kills bacteria on food
anus	food leaves the gut here
oesophagus	delivers food to the stomach
mouth	teeth chew food; saliva begins starch digestion
large intestine	absorption of water
small intestine	continues digestion and site of absorption of food

GCSE-style questions
1. Larger surface area for the enzyme to act on
2. **a)** sugars (e.g. glucose)
   b) **Any two from:** to increase the solubility of molecules; to make food small enough to be absorbed and transported in the blood; to provide raw materials for synthesis
3. **Any two from:** large surface area provided by folds; villi; and microvilli; long length
4. diffusion
5. capillaries
6. **a)** liver **b)** hepatic portal vein **c)** urea
7. mouth; oesophagus; stomach; small intestine; large intestine; anus.

Pages 30–31 Distance, Speed and Velocity

Multiple-choice questions
1. B   2. C   3. C   4. A   5. C

Short-answer questions
1. 5 m/s
2. 3; **A** 4; **B** 2; **C** 1; **D**

GCSE-style questions
1. $330 \times 4 = 1320$ m (**1 mark for calculation; 1 mark for answer**)
2. a) $\frac{400}{50} = 8$ m/s (**1 mark for calculation; 1 mark for answer**)
   b) 0 m/s; velocity is a vector and the displacement after a whole lap is zero.
3. a) 3 m/s $\times$ 60 s = 180 m (**1 mark for calculation; 1 mark for answer**)
   b)

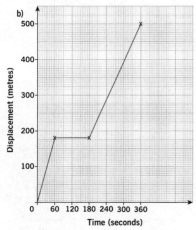

(**1 mark for scale and label on *y*-axis; 1 mark for scale and label on *x*-axis; 1 mark for accurately plotted points; 1 mark for line of graph.**)
   c) $\frac{500\text{ m} - 180\text{ m}}{180\text{ s}} = \frac{320\text{ m}}{180\text{ s}} = 1.8$ m/s (**1 mark for calculation; 1 mark for answer**)
   d) $\frac{500\text{ m}}{(6 \times 60\text{ s})} = \frac{500\text{ m}}{360\text{ s}} = 1.4$ m/s (**1 mark for calculation; 1 mark for answer**)

Pages 32–33 Speed, Velocity and Acceleration

Multiple-choice questions
1. B   2. B   3. B   4. A   5. B

Short-answer questions
1. **A** travelling at a constant velocity
   B decelerating
   C travelling at a lower constant velocity
   D accelerating
   E stationary
2. Indication of a stationary object – Horizontal line on distance–time graph; Acceleration – Gradient of velocity–time graph; Distance travelled – area under velocity–time graph; Velocity – gradient of distance–time graph.

GCSE-style questions
1. a)

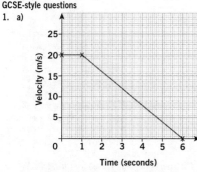

(**1 mark for scale and label on *y*-axis; 1 mark for scale and label on *x*-axis; 1 mark for accurately plotted points; 1 mark for line of graph.**)
   b) i)   area under the graph for the first second shaded and labelled thinking distance
      ii) 20 m
   c) i)   area under the graph between 1 and 6 seconds shaded and labelled braking distance.
      ii) $\frac{20 \times 5}{2} = 50$ m

---

d) $\frac{20\text{m/s}}{5\text{ s}} = 4$ m/s^2
   e) The line would have a steeper slope (greater gradient).
2. a) Change of speed = 17.2 – 4.5 = 12.7 m/s; acceleration = $\frac{12.7}{2.5}$ = 5.08 m/s^2 = 5.1 m/s^2 (2 s.f.)
   b) A horizontal straight line.

Pages 34–35 Forces

Multiple-choice questions
1. D   2. B   3. C   4. A   5. C

Short-answer questions
1. a) weight
   b) Newtons
   c) ...all objects remain at rest or move at constant velocity (speed in a straight line); unless acted upon by a resultant external force.
2. a) Diagram of aircraft with arrows showing vertical forces – weight down; lift upwards; horizontal forces – thrust forwards; drag (air resistance) backwards.
   b) lift = weight; thrust = drag
   c) 10 000 N (10 kN)

GCSE-style questions
1. a) 700 N b)i) mass is 70 kg ii) weight is 119 N
2. a)

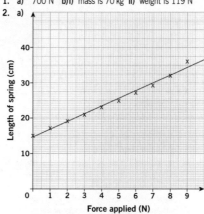

(**1 mark for scale and label on *y*-axis; 1 mark for scale and label on *x*-axis; 1 mark for accurately plotted points; 1 mark for line of graph.**)
   b) 22.0 cm (+ or – 0.1 cm)
   c) total length of spring = 15 + 11.5 = 26.5; using graph force (weight)
      = 5.7N (+ or – 0.1N); mass = $\frac{\text{weight}}{g}$ = 0.57 kg

Pages 36–37 Acceleration and Momentum

Multiple-choice questions
1. B   2. C   3. B   4. D   5. A

Short-answer questions
1. a) The trolley starts to move, accelerating at a constant rate.
   b) i) The trolley would accelerate more gently.
      ii) The trolley would accelerate more quickly.
2. mass $\times$ acceleration; rate of change of momentum.

GCSE-style questions
1. a) Velocity = acceleration $\times$ time; 7 m/s (**1 mark for calculation; 1 mark for answer**)
   b) 280 kgm/s
   c) f = $\frac{280}{0.2}$ = 1400 N (**1 mark for calculation; 1 mark for answer**)
   d) Increasing the time reduces the force exerted on his body; there is therefore less likelihood of injury
2. a) Driver's initial momentum = 2100 kgm/s; 21 000 N
   b) Airbag / seatbelt
   c) Data showing reduced incidence of fatal injuries to drivers in road accidents; whether a seatbelt (or airbag) was used / speed of vehicle.

Pages 38–39 Pairs of Forces: Action and Reaction

Multiple-choice questions
1. B   2. B   3. B   4. C   5. C

Short-answer questions
1. velocity; the same; conserved; force; short; longer; size; opposite; action; reaction.

---

1. a) Arrow from centre of Earth towards centre of Moon; arrow from centre of Moon towards centre of Earth; arrows of equivalent length
   b) The forces have the same magnitude; but act in opposite directions.
   c) Arrow from centre of person towards centre of Earth; arrow from centre of Earth towards centre of person; arrows of equivalent length.
2. a) momentum of car = 1000 $\times$ speed; momentum of truck = 2500 $\times$ speed in opposite direction; total momentum = 1500 $\times$ speed in direction of truck.
   b) total momentum = 22 500 kgm/s; total mass = 3500 kg; velocity = 6.4 m/s; in original direction of truck.

Pages 40–41 Work and Energy

Multiple-choice questions
1. C   2. C   3. A   4. A   5. B

Short-answer questions
1. a) Mass $\times$ gravitational field strength $\times$ height = 225 000 J (**1 mark for calculation; 1 mark for answer**)
   b)

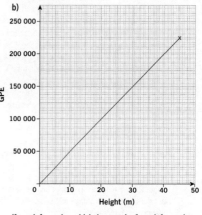

(**1 mark for scale and label on *y*-axis; 1 mark for scale and label on *x*-axis; 1 mark for line of graph.**)
   c) i) Potential energy at half height = 112 500 J; Kinetic energy on impact = 112 500 J
      ii) $\frac{1}{2} \times$ mass $\times$ velocity^2 = 112 500; 21.2 m/s

GCSE-style questions
1. a) ✎ At point 1, the rollercoaster has gravitational potential energy (GPE) but no kinetic energy (KE) because it is stationary. As it falls down the first drop, GPE transfers to KE so at point 2 the rollercoaster has less GPE than at the start, plus some KE. At point 3, the rollercoaster has the minimum GPE and maximum KE. As the roller coaster begins to climb the loop at point 4, some of this KE transfers to GPE.
   b) the starting height; energy.
   c) GPE change = mass $\times$ g $\times$ change in height; KE = GPE change; 875 kJ
   d) $\frac{1}{2} \times$ mass $\times$ velocity^2 = 875 000; 26.5 m/s
   e) mass $\times$ g $\times$ change of height = ½ $\times$ mass $\times$ velocity^2; therefore velocity is independent of mass; so there would be no change to answer d).

Pages 42–43 Energy and Power

Multiple-choice questions
1. B   2. B   3. A   4. C   5. B

Short-answer questions
1. a) 100 N $\times$ 10 m = 1000 J
   b) $\frac{100\text{ J}}{4\text{ s}}$ = 250 W
2. a)

(**1 mark**)
(**1 mark**)
(**1 mark**)

   b) balanced; terminal.

Answers

GCSE-style questions

1. **a)** Gain in GPE = 744 J; KE increases by 744 J in 1.2 s; 620 W (J/s)
   b) GPE increases by 744 J in 6 s; 124 W
2. **a)** 80 km/h = 22.2 m/s; KE = 740 kJ
   b) Work done = force × distance = 740 000; 7400 N
   c) **i)** thinking distance = speed × thinking time; 20 m
      ii) Braking distance reduced to 80 m; 9250 N
   d) **i)** driver's alertness
      ii) **Any one from:** road conditions; brake or tyre condition; vehicle load.
      iii) speed

Pages 44–45 Electrostatic Effects

Multiple-choice questions
1. C **2.** D **3.** B **4.** B
Short-answer questions
1. Electrons; balloon; opposite; opposite; attraction.
2. The conductor must be fully insulated; otherwise the electrons readily flow to and from the conductor, preventing charge build up.
GCSE-style questions
1. **a)** ✎ In this experiment, the flour passes through the apparatus in the same way as it would in a flour mill. The flour slides down the chute and the friction against the surface of the chute causes a charge transfer. Charged flour builds up in the can, as indicated by the electroscope. The chute retains the opposite charge. In the same way, flour moving along chutes in a mill, results in an accumulating static charge separation.
   b) If the charge separation builds up sufficiently it will discharge with a spark; this spark could be sufficient to ignite a combustible material.
   c) A conductor can be connected between the chute and the can; this will safely discharge the static before it can build up sufficiently to pose a hazard.
   d) **Answers may include:** The refuelling of aircraft has the potential for charge separation in a combustible environment; connecting the plane and the tanker, or earthing both, prevents the charge from building up.

Pages 46–47 Uses of Electrostatics

Multiple-choice questions
1. A **2.** D **3.** A **4.** C **5.** B
Short-answer questions
1. negative; the same; repel; attracted; opposite; even; away.
2. The charge flows through the patient's chest between the defibrillator plates; The flow of charge causes the heart muscles to contract; This is used to treat patients with cardiac arrhythmia or whose hearts have stopped.
GCSE-style questions
1. **a)** A 3; B 1; C 5; D 2; E 4; F 6.
   b) The paper would need to be positively charged; the opposite charge will attract the toner to the paper.
2. Smoke particles in the exhaust stream pass through a charged grid; the particles become charged; the charged particles are attracted to the oppositely charged plates lining the walls of the chimney; the particles stick to the plates and clump together.

Pages 48–49 Electric Circuits

Multiple-choice questions
1. B **2.** C **3.** D **4.** A
Short-answer questions
1. charge; continuous; current; electrons; positive; negative; amps; the same as.
2. **a)** 500 mA **b)** 1.5 A **c)** 0.6 A
GCSE-style questions
1. **a) and b)**   X

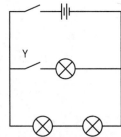

c) If B can be switched off then there would be no current flowing through B; therefore, no current flowing through C as they are on the same piece of wire.
d) The branch of the circuit with Bulbs B and C has twice the resistance of that with Bulb A; therefore, the current through B and C is 0.1 A; the total current is the sum of the currents through each branch; so it is 0.3 A.
e)

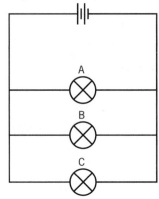

f) Each bulb now has a current of 0.2 A; total current is therefore 0.8 A.

Pages 50–51 Voltage or Potential Difference

Multiple-choice questions
1. D **2.** B **3.** C **4.** A **5.** B
Short-answer questions
1. **a)** true **b)** true **c)** false **d)** true **e)** true **f)** false
2. **a)** $A_3 = 0.2$ A **b)** $A_4 = 0.3$ A **c)** $V_2 = 3$ V **d)** $V_3 = 3$ V
GCSE-style questions
1. **a)** One circuit diagram showing the two bulbs in series; correct symbols must be used; one circuit diagram showing the two bulbs in parallel; correct symbols must be used.
   b) In the series circuit, both bulbs will be of equivalent brightness because they have the same current; in the parallel circuit, both bulbs will be of equivalent brightness because they have the same potential difference; the bulbs in series circuit will be less bright than those in the parallel circuit because the potential difference is divided between the bulbs.
   c) **i)** **Answers may include:** something wrong with one of the components; user error.
      ii) The student should repeat the experiment.
   d) **i)** series **ii)** parallel
   e) 1.5 V = 1.5 J/C; charge for 0.3 J = 0.2 C; 0.2 C/s = 0.2 A.

Pages 52–53 Resistance and Resistors

Multiple-choice questions
1. A **2.** C **3.** C **4.** B **5.** D
Short-answer questions
1. **a)** the free electrons
   b) The electrons are free to move if a potential difference is applied – free electrons move from negative to positive (actual current)
   c) In an insulator the electrons are tightly bound and not able to move if a potential difference is applied.
2. **a)** 0.3 A
   b) the current would fall to 0.15 A
   c) the current would increase to 0.6 A
GCSE-style questions
1. **a)** the lattice of ions
   b) electrons collide with the lattice ions and lose energy; the ions vibrate more, causing an increase in temperature
   c) resistance is the voltage per unit current; it is measured in ohms
2. **a)** 125 mA
   b) first bulb = 1 V; second bulb = 2 V
   c) **i)** first bulb = 375 mA; second bulb = 188 mA.
      ii) total current = 0.56 A; effective resistance = 5.3 Ω.

Pages 54–55 Special Resistors

Multiple-choice questions
1. C **2.** C **3.** A **4.** C **5.** C

Short-answer questions
1. **a)** As the filament temperature increases, the lattice ions vibrate more; this results in an increase in its resistance.
   b) In a thermistor, resistance decreases with increasing temperature.
   c)

   Current

   Voltage

   Original line

   New line

GCSE-style questions
1. **a)** **i)** 10 Ω **ii)** 12 Ω
   b) Non-Ohmic; because current is not directly proportional to applied voltage.
   c)

   Current

   Voltage

   (1 mark for: current flow in forward direction for voltage above a threshold; 1 mark for: no current for reverse polarity; 1 mark for: steep gradient when current flowing in forward direction.)
   d) To prevent current flow in one particular direction.
2. Resistance is dependent on the amount of light falling on the LDR; the greater the intensity, the less resistance.

Pages 56–57 The Mains Supply

Multiple-choice questions
1. C **2.** B **3.** B **4.** A **5.** A
Short-answer questions
1. **a)** 1 = earth wire; 2 = neutral wire; 3 = live wire; 4 = cable grip; 5 = fuse.
   b) Safety device that limits the current that can flow; current exceeding the rating causes heating sufficient to melt the thin wire within the fuse.
   c) 13 × 230 = 2990 W; 3.0 kW
GCSE-style questions
1. **a)** Earthing involves ensuring all exposed metal parts are connected to Earth; if a fault develops and the live wire touches any of these parts a large current flows safely to Earth; additionally, the fuse will melt ('blow') and cut the electricity supply.
   b) If there are no exposed metal parts then earthing is unnecessary as the user cannot come into contact with the live current; this is called double insulation.
2. **a)** Residual current is caused by a difference in the currents in the live and neutral wires, indicating a leakage to earth.
   b) The RCCB 'trips' (breaks the circuit) if this current is excessive; preventing the operator from receiving an electric shock.
   c) A circuit breaker is more sensitive than a fuse; and responds much more rapidly when a problem occurs.

Pages 58–59 Atomic Structure

Multiple-choice questions
1. C **2.** A **3.** D **4.** D **5.** B
Short-answer questions
1. **a)** electron: $\frac{1}{1840}$, –1; proton: 1, +1; neutron: 1, 0

b) The number of electrons is equal to the number of protons.
2. a) 26 protons, 30 neutrons, 26 electrons
   b) 15 protons, 17 neutrons, 15 electrons
   c) 19 protons, 20 neutrons, 18 electrons

GCSE-style questions
1. a) The atom is made of positively charged material; it is embedded with negatively charged electrons; diagram should show a 'solid' looking sphere (pudding), studded with negative particles.
   b) C; E.
2. a) Isotopes of an element all have the same number of protons / atomic number; there are two different atomic numbers (7 and 8).
   b) Isotopes are atoms of the same element with the same number of protons; and with varying numbers of neutrons (and therefore mass).
3. $^{218}_{84}$Po

Pages 60–61 Radioactive Decay

Multiple-choice questions
1. C   2. C   3. B   4. D   5. B
Short-answer questions
1. a) false b) true c) false d) true e) true f) false
2. a) 4000 Bq
   b) $4000 \div 2 \div 2 \div 2 = 500$ Bq (1 mark for calculation; 1 mark for answer)

GCSE-style questions
1. a) Sam would get no change in the reading for both beta and gamma if a material like paper was used; the reading would partially decrease if a sheet of aluminium a few mm think (or similar) was used because beta would stop; the reading would drop to almost zero if several cm of lead or a substantial thickness of concrete would be used as this is necessary to stop gamma readings.
   b) **Any two from:** handle materials with tongs; wear protective clothing; limit exposure time to the materials; (Accept any other sensible answer.)
   c) The time taken for half the radioactive atoms (or nuclei) to decay / for the activity to fall by half.
   d) 🖉 The half-life of an isotope is the average time taken for half the nuclei present to decay. As it an average, some atoms will decay faster and some will decay slower than the rate given as the half-life. Therefore, it is impossible to say when, exactly, an individual atom will decay. Both statements are true in this respect.
   e) False (external conditions do not affect the intrinsic decay rate)

Pages 62–63 Living with Radioactivity

Multiple-choice questions
1. B   2. C   3. D   4. D   5. B
Short-answer questions
1. a) Some of the elements present in our food have naturally occurring radioisotopes; Exposure of food to radiation does not make it radioactive.
   b) If our food is contaminated then we will take excess radioactive material into our bodies; Irradiation from within our bodies will result in much greater exposure / energy absorption and damage to our cells than exposure from outside.

GCSE-style questions
1. a) radiation that occurs in the environment.
   b) granite rock releases radon gas; radon can accumulate within closed spaces (such as buildings).
   c) 🖉 If radon gas is inhaled, it will then decay in the lungs. The decay process results in deposits of radioactive material. As a result, the lungs will be exposed to significant irradiation from within, leading to an increased risk of lung cancer.
2. a) 24 hours later is 13 half-lives; the activity will therefore drop by a factor of 2^{13} (i.e. 8192-fold).
   b) The background activity is approximately 2 Bq; this should be subtracted from the initial activity of 212 Bq.

Pages 64–65 Uses of Radioactive Materials

Multiple-choice questions
1. C   2. A   3. D   4. B   5. C
Short-answer questions
1. Smoke particles reduce the number of alpha particles reaching the detector so the alarm is triggered; Beta and gamma emissions are unsuitable as they would pass through the smoke.
2. Gamma; since the radiation must pass through a substantial thickness of soil.

GCSE-style questions
1. a) The level of activity reaching the detector is dependent on the thickness of the foil.
   b) Beta
   c) Steel would absorb too much beta radiation; so gamma would be more appropriate.
   d) Long half-life; so that the activity remains constant throughout the production process.
2. Exposure to radiation can potentially damage cells in the body or cause cancers to develop and so should be minimised for a healthy person; For a person who already has cancer the small risk of exposure is outweighed by the useful information gained to inform treatment planning.

Pages 66–67 Nuclear Fission and Fusion

Multiple-choice questions
1. C   2. D   3. C   4. B   5. B
Short-answer questions
1. a) i) fuel rods   ii) moderator
      iii) reactor core   iv) coolant
      v) turbines   vi) neutrons
   b) Low level waste – Sealed into containers and put in landfill sites; Intermediate level waste – Mixed with concrete and stored in stainless steel containers; High level waste – Kept under water in cooling tanks.

GCSE-style questions
1. a) Repulsion
   b) i) high temperature; high pressure.
      ii) The fuel needed is hydrogen, which can be obtained from water; no radioactive waste is created.
2. a) $^{141}_{56}$Ba + $^{92}_{36}$Kr
   b) 2 neutrons
   c) $^{235}_{92}$U + $^{1}_{0}$n $\longrightarrow$ $^{140}_{54}$Xe + $^{94}_{38}$Sr + 2^{1}_{0}n
      (1 mark for each correct product)

Pages 68–69 Stars

Multiple-choice questions
1. A   2. D   3. B   4. C   5. D
Short-answer questions
1. a) gravitational force
   b) The radiation and kinetic energy of the material inside the star exerts an outward pressure; this balances the gravitational attraction.
2. A gas cloud   B main sequence
   C red supergiant   D supernova
   E neutron star or black hole

GCSE-style questions
1. a) 🖉 A star starts to become unstable when the hydrogen nuclei that 'fuel' fusion start to run out. In a small star, like our Sun, the star cools, becoming redder, and expands to form a red giant. The core contracts and the outer are layers are lost (forming the planetary nebula). The remaining core becomes a hot and dense white dwarf, which will eventually cool to become a black dwarf.
   b) As a very massive star swells it forms a red supergiant; that eventually explodes (a supernova); the collapse of the red supergiant core can lead to a neutron star or even a black hole after the supernova explosion.
2. The core of a star must be many millions of degrees so that the hydrogen nuclei have enough kinetic energy; to overcome their repulsion and fuse to form helium nuclei; releasing energy as electromagnetic radiation.
3. $1604 - 20\,000 = -18\,396$, explosion occurred in 18 396 BC

Pages 70–71 Atomic Structure

Multiple-choice questions
1. B   2. C   3. B   4. B   5. C
Short-answer questions
1. electrons; neutrons; protons; 1; electrons; neutrons; protons; electrons; neutrons; isotopes
2. a) 1   b) 1
   c) tritium has one more neutron

GCSE-style questions
1.

	Relative mass	Relative charge	Where found in the atom
Electron	$\frac{1}{1840}$	–1	shells
Proton	1	+1	nucleus
Neutron	1	0	nucleus

2. a) i) proton   ii) neutron   iii) electron
   b) the orbits around a nucleus; in which the electrons are found.
   c) mass number = protons + neutrons = 3 + 4 = 7 atomic number = number of protons = 3
   d) $^{7}_{3}$Li

Pages 72–76 Atoms and the Periodic Table

Multiple-choice questions
1. C   2. A   3. D   4. C   5. D
Short-answer questions
1. group number is the same as the number of electrons; in the outer shell.
2. two in the first shell; one in the second shell.
3. the number of positive protons and the number of negative electrons are equal; so the charges cancel out.
4. eight electrons

GCSE-style questions
1. a) six   b) in the nucleus
   c) the atom has six protons; and six electrons.
   d) on the diagram: two in the first shell; four in the second.
   e) group 4; period 2.
   f) intermediate properties as elements in group 4 have intermediate properties.
2. in the nucleus, protons have a mass of 1 amu; neutrons have a mass of 1 amu; electrons outside the nucleus have negligible mass (OWTTE).

Pages 74–75 The Periodic Table

Multiple-choice questions
1. C   2. C   3. D   4. A   5. A
Short-answer questions
1. a)

Property	Sulfur	Selenium	Tellurium
Relative atomic mass	32	79	**126**
Boiling point (°C)	445	**716**	987

   b) Dobereiner   c) density
   d) the pattern only seemed to work some of the time

GCSE-style questions
1. a) D and G   b) C and D   c) F   d) D
   e) H   f) E   g) B   h) J
   i) J   j) I   k) A
   l) G and H
   m) i) same number of electrons in the outer energy level (shell)
      ii) G has one more shell
   n) i) same number of shells
      ii) G has more electrons in outer shell

Pages 76–77 Chemical Reactions and Atoms

Multiple-choice questions
1. D   2. A   3. B   4. C   5. D
Short-answer questions
1. nitrogen, hydrogen, oxygen; ratio 1:5:1.
2. ionic bonding; because a metal is bonded to a non-metal.
3. a compound; because there are two capital letters, so two different elements.

4. allow 1 mark for hydrogen and oxygen, but two marks for water: H_2O
5. it has lost; two electrons.

GCSE-style questions
1. a) all are compounds; containing just two elements
   b) NaCl and CuO; because they are compounds of a metal and a non-metal.
   c) CO_2 and SO_2; because both have two oxygen atoms to one of the other element.
   d) **Any two from:** tells the scientist which elements are present; tells the scientist the ratio of atoms of each element; the formula is the same in all languages.
   e) nitrogen and hydrogen have combined; in the ratio 1:3.

Pages 78–79 Balancing Equations

Multiple-choice questions
1. B 2. B 3. A 4. A 5. C

Short-answer questions
1. a)   2   2
   b)   –   –   2
   c)   –   2   –   2
   d)   –   3   2
   e)   –   2   –   2
   f)   3   2   3   3   –

GCSE-style questions
1. 1. products
   2. atoms; sides
   3. number; one
   4. state
2. a) 6 moles of oxygen; 6 moles of carbon dioxide and 6 moles of water
   b) i) 6 carbon, 12 hydrogen, 18 oxygen
      ii) 6 carbon, 12 hydrogen, 18 oxygen
   c) The equation balances; there are the same number of each kind of atom on both sides of the equation.

Pages 80–81 Ionic and Covalent Bonding

Multiple-choice questions
1. B 2. D 3. A 4. C 5. B

Short-answer questions
1. a) i) 1   ii) 6   iii) 4   iv) 4
   b)

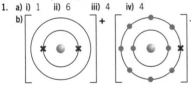

Li   **F**

(transfer of electron from lithium to fluorine shown; correct electronic structure of ions; charges on ions.)

GCSE-style questions
1. a) hydrogen; carbon; nitrogen
   b) i) 1   ii) 4   iii) 3
   c) triple
2. a) i) solid, ionic compound **(both required for 1 mark)**
      ii) conduct when molten; soluble in water
   b) metal, it forms ionic bonds **(both required for 1 mark)**
   c) i) 2+   ii) YO
   d)

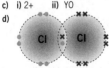

(1 mark for (•×) in overlap; 2 marks for each atom having 8 electrons)

Pages 82–83 Ionic and Covalent Structures

Multiple-choice questions
1. D 2. B 3. C 4. B 5. D

Short-answer questions
1. a) calcium carbonate and potassium chloride
   b) neon
   c) carbon dioxide and methane
   d) carbon dioxide and methane
   e) diamond
   f) potassium chloride

GCSE-style questions
1. a) 4
   b) magnesium + silicon dioxide ⟶ magnesium oxide + silicon
      $2Mg(s) + SiO_2(s) \longrightarrow 2MgO(s) + Si(s)$
   c) i)

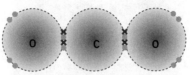

(1 mark for each correct electron number)

(1 mark for 2 double bonds; 1 mark for other electrons)

      ii) $2Mg + O_2 \longrightarrow 2MgO$
          $C + O_2 \longrightarrow CO_2$
      iii) CO_2 has a simple molecular structure; MgO is a giant ionic lattice
   d) MgO has strong electrostatic attraction; between oppositely charged ions; carbon dioxide has weak forces between molecules.
   e) it would need to be molten

Pages 84–85 Group 7

Multiple-choice questions
1. A 2. D 3. D 4. B 5. A

Short-answer questions
1. X_2 is bromine, Y_2 is iodine, Z_2 is chlorine **(1 mark for 1 or 2 correct; 2 marks for all 3 correct)**

GCSE-style questions
1. a) row 1: fluorine; any value less than 90 pm
      row 2: 2, 8, 7
      row 3: any value less than 0°C
      row 4: I; any value more than 150°C
   b) bromine; room temperature lies between the melting and boiling point
   c) iodine; it has the most electrons
   d) period 4; it has 4 energy levels (shells)
2. a) i) 117   ii) 177   iii) 117
   b) 588   c) 7   d) –1   e) solid   f) no reaction

Pages 86–87 New Chemicals and Materials

Multiple-choice questions
1. B 2. D 3. A 4. C 5. A

Short-answer questions
1. sulfuric acid; ammonia.
2. Many medicines are only required in relatively small quantities; continuous processes are used to produce bulk quantities and would result in waste.
3. if people working with nanoparticles do not cover their skin; nanoparticles may enter the bloodstream and could be toxic
4. very strong; covalent bonds
5. A ball-shaped molecule formed of carbon atoms; (each carbon atom is joined to three others) joined together to form hexagonal and pentagonal faces.

GCSE-style questions
1. a) it is difficult to reach the windows; and unsafe for window cleaners
   b) it has to be transparent; and the coating is expensive
   c) speeds up the reaction; when activated by sunlight
   d) it is expensive; and it is not hard to clean windows of ordinary houses
   e) it will protect the people inside from ultraviolet light; which can cause skin cancer

Pages 88–89 Plastics and Perfumes

Multiple-choice questions
1. B 2. D 3. A 4. D 5. D

Short-answer questions
1. **Any two from:** cotton; wood; leather; silk; wool **(or other sensible answer).**
2. **Any one from:** polyethene from ethene; polypropene from propene; PVC from vinyl chloride; PTFE (Teflon) from tetrafluoroethene

3. crystallinity increases rigidity; and it makes the plastic more brittle
4. it has very low friction; and food will not stick to it
5. So that the body heat causes it to evaporate; and carry the scent through the air.

GCSE-style questions
1. a) ethene molecules are made to join together; at high pressure with a catalyst
   b) they must be melted
   c) polythene is thermoplastic; as it has to be heated to soften it
   d) **Any two from:** the bucket is cheaper; lighter; will not corrode
   e) the plasticiser makes the bucket more flexible; and less likely to crack; if dropped or overloaded

Pages 90–91 Analysis

Multiple-choice questions
1. B 2. B 3. D 4. A 5. C

Short-answer questions
1. qualitative identifies what is present; quantitative measures how much
2. distance moved by the spot; divided by distance moved by the solvent
3. substances that are insoluble in water; need other solvents that they will dissolve in
4. the time taken for a component to pass through the column of the chromatogram.

GCSE-style questions
1. a) because the prohibited substance may pass out of the body very quickly; so it cannot be detected after a time
   b) so that the sample cannot be contaminated; or confused with samples from other athletes
   c) i) gas chromatography–mass spectrometry
      ii) different substances have different retention times; as the sample passes through the machine, depending on their attraction to the stationary phase
   d) the peak may be masked by the peak of another substance which may not be prohibited
   e) modern analytical techniques are much more sensitive; and can detect more substances and much lower concentrations

Pages 92–93 Metals

Multiple-choice questions
1. A 2. D 3. B 4. D 5. C

Short-answer questions
1. giant structures
2. the metallic bonding is very strong; so it needs a lot of energy to break the bonds
3. vibration of the metal atoms; increases the electrical resistance
4. **Any one from:** a shape-memory alloy; smart alloy
5. electrons that are free to move; between atoms
6. electric current is a flow of electrons; free electrons can flow through the structure

GCSE-style questions
1. a) one picture shows all atoms the same; the other has two different types of atom
   b) 24-carat gold ring is more expensive; because gold is more expensive than copper;
   c) 9-carat gold would be stronger; as it is an alloy
   d) by calculating the density of each ring; 24-carat gold is more dense
   e) a harder gold ring will wear away a softer gold ring; usually damaging the more expensive ring

Pages 94–95 Group 1

Multiple-choice questions
1. B 2. A 3. C 4. B 5. D

Short-answer questions
1. a) i) 2, 1   ii) lower   iii) larger
   b) all have one electron in their outer shell
   c) 19

GCSE-style questions
1. a) less reactive
   b) i) lithium oxide   ii) lithium chloride
   c) i) hydrogen
      ii) it would turn red litmus paper blue

iii) lithium + water ⟶ lithium hydroxide + hydrogen **(1 mark for each product)**

d) i) Li⁺

ii) the ion has lost; one electron

iii) Li ⟶ Li⁺ + e⁻ **(1 mark for each product)**

e) ✎ Lithium fluoride is a group 1 halide, therefore it will have properties similar to sodium chloride. It will be a white solid that is soluble in water to form a colourless solution. It will conduct electricity when molten or when in aqueous solution.

Pages 96–97 Aluminium and Transition Metals

Multiple-choice questions
1. A 2. A 3. B 4. A 5. D

Short-answer questions
1. a) It is positive.
   b) It stays the same colour; Copper ions are formed at the anode; at the same rate as they are deposited at the cathode.

GCSE-style questions
1. a) using electricity to break down or decompose; a compound
   b) Al³⁺; O²⁻; Na⁺
   c) reduction is the removal of oxygen; aluminium oxide has been reduced to aluminium.
   d) i) cheaper electricity.
      ii) stops heat energy escaping.

Pages 98–99 Chemical Tests

Multiple-choice questions
1. A 2. C 3. C 4. A 5. B

Short-answer questions
1. barium — light green
   calcium — red
   lithium — crimson
   sodium — yellow
2. a) silver bromide   b) Br⁻/bromide ion.

GCSE-style questions
1. a) i) Clean a nichrome wire by placing it in the hottest part of the Bunsen burner / dipping it in hydrochloric acid; Dip the end of the wire into (water then) the salt sample; Hold the salt in the hottest part of the Bunsen flame and observe the colour.
      ii) **Any two from:** wear goggles; wear heat-proof gloves; where a lab jacket; perform test in a fume cabinet (any other sensible answer).
      iii) The salt contains potassium ions.
   b) i) To see if the salt contained halide ions.
      ii) Chloride; bromide; and iodide compounds.
   c) Potassium sulfate.

Pages 100–101 Acids and Bases

Multiple-choice questions
1. A 2. D 3. D 4. C 5. A

Short-answer questions
1. a) true b) false c) false d) true e) false
   f) false g) true

GCSE-style questions
1. a) i) ⟶ ii) ⇌
   b) A – slow reaction
      B – carbon dioxide given off
      C – allow 3–5
   c) i) more than is required to react completely
      ii) same volume as both acids are in excess; volume will depend on mass of sodium carbonate
   d) i) hydrochloric acid
      ii) ethanoic acid
2. a) **Any one from:** sodium hydroxide; potassium hydroxide (or other suitable answer)
   b) i) making soap; dyeing fabric (mordant)
      ii) making fertilisers

Pages 102–103 Making Salts

Multiple-choice questions
1. B 2. A 3. C 4. D 5. B

Short-answer questions
1. HCl + NaOH ⟶ NaCl + H₂O **(1 mark for products; 1 mark for balanced equation)**
2. calcium nitrate; and water
3. by filtration
4. a) H⁺ b) OH⁻ c) H⁺(aq) + OH ⟶ H₂O

GCSE-style questions
1. a) an acid should be placed in the burette
   b) to increase the surface area of the solid; making the neutralisation faster
   c) crushed tablet and an indicator
   d) acid added, gradually; until the indicator changed colour. Volume of acid added measured and recorded.
   e) **Any two from:** must not be toxic or produce anything toxic; must not have any unwanted side effects; pleasant taste; reaction with acid not too exothermic

Pages 104–105 Metal Carbonate Reactions

Multiple-choice questions
1. C 2. C 3. B 4. C 5. B

Short-answer questions
1. a) sodium chloride; NaCl
      magnesium sulfate; MgSO₄
      zinc nitrate; Zn(NO₃)₂
      calcium ethanoate; (CH₃COO)₂Ca
      potassium phosphate; K₃PO₄
   b) carbon dioxide; water

GCSE-style questions
1. a) i) carbon dioxide   ii) exothermic
      iii) to speed up the rate of reaction/provide a large surface area
   b) i) no carbon dioxide given off/no bubbles
      ii) green solid left, which does not react any more
   c) to remove excess copper(II) carbonate
   d) i) the liquid that has passed through the filter paper
      ii) a solution that contains as much dissolved substance as possible at a particular temperature
   e) water vapour
   f) i) copper(II) carbonate + sulfuric acid ⟶ copper(II) sulfate + carbon dioxide + water
      ii) CuCO₃(s) + H₂SO₄(aq) ⟶ CuSO₄(aq) + CO₂(g) + H₂O(l) **(1 mark for reactants; 1 mark for products)**

Pages 106–107 The Electrolysis of Sodium Chloride Solution

Multiple-choice questions
1. B 2. D 3. C 4. A 5. C

Short-answer questions
1. it lowers the melting point of ice, causing ice to melt
2. hydrogen; oxygen
3. the solid must melt to allow the ions to move
4. reduction
5. oxidation

GCSE-style questions
1. a) hydrogen; chlorine
   b) they lose electrons to become atoms; which join together to make Cl₂ molecules
   c) sodium hydroxide is produced; sodium hydroxide solution is alkaline
   d) 2H⁺ + 2e⁻ ⟶ H₂ **(1 mark for products, 1 mark for balanced equation)**
   e) **Any two from:** bleach; PVC; water sterilisers; hydrochloric acid; HCFCs

Pages 108–109 Relative Formula Mass and Percentage Composition

Multiple-choice questions
1. C 2. D 3. C 4. C 5. A

Short-answer questions
1. a) the average mass of an atom; compared to one-twelfth the mass of an atom of carbon-12
   b) the sum of the relative atomic masses of each atom; in a molecule
2. a) i) 80   ii) 158; 160; 162
   b) ³⁵Cl; the average value is nearer this isotope than ³⁷Cl

GCSE-style questions
1. a) i)

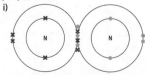

(1 mark for diagram showing triple covalent bond; 1 mark for rest of diagram correct)

ii) triple bond is very difficult to break

b) i) 40 + 12 + (3 × 16) = 100 **(1 mark for correct calculation; 1 mark for answer)**
   ii) 3 × 24 + n × 14 = 100 **(alternative approaches also gain mark if answer is correct)**
      14n = 28   n = 2
   iii) $\frac{72}{100}$; 72%

c) ammonia d) alkali (allow base or soluble base)

e) i) magnesium nitride + water ⟶ magnesium hydroxide + ammonia **(1 mark for reactants; 1 mark for products)**
   ii) $\frac{10}{100}$; 0.1
   iii) Mg₃N₂(s) + 6H₂O(l) ⟶ 3Mg(OH)₂(aq) + 2NH₃(g) **(1 mark for correct formulae; 1 mark for balanced equation)**

Pages 110–111 Calculating Masses

Multiple-choice questions
1. B 2. D 3. B 4. D 5. C

Short-answer questions
1. a) 1.5 b) 0.7 c) 0.25 d) 0.1 e) 0.01

GCSE-style questions
1. a) i) 0.4 × 5; = 2 moles   ii) 2 moles
   b) i) alkene ii) C₂H₄
      iii) C₂H₄(g) + 3O₂(g) ⟶ 2CO₂(g) + 2H₂O(g) (also accept 2H₂O(l)) **(1 mark for correct formulae; 1 mark for balanced equation)**
2. a) 10 × 63; = 630g
   b) $\frac{472.5}{630}$ × 100; = 75%

Pages 112–113 Rates of Reaction

Multiple-choice questions
1. A 2. D 3. B 4. B 5. D

Short-answer questions
1. activation; catalyst; temperature; surface; pressure; closer; concentration; collisions

GCSE-style questions
1. a)

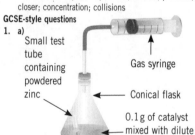

Small test tube containing powdered zinc

Gas syringe

Conical flask

0.1g of catalyst mixed with dilute sulfuric acid

(1 mark for showing method for keeping chemicals separated; 1 mark for gas syringe; 1 mark for connecting tube; 1 mark for correctly labelled)

b) Zn(s) + H₂SO₄(aq) ⟶ ZnSO₄(aq) + H₂(g) **(1 mark for correct formulae; 1 mark for balanced equation with state symbols)**
c) hydrogen burns with a 'pop' when a lighted splint is applied
d) i) copper ii) as the control iii) temperature
e) copper powder has greater surface area than copper lumps

Pages 114–115 Reversible Reactions

Multiple-choice questions
1. D 2. A 3. B 4. C 5. B

Short-answer questions
1. completion; products; reactants; endothermic; ammonia; hydrogen chloride; ammonium chloride

GCSE-style questions
1. a) the forward and reverse reactions are happening at the same rate; so there are no changes in concentrations
   b) **Any one from:** blue litmus will turn red/pH-meter would show a decrease in pH
   c) The forward reaction must be endothermic; An increase in temperature will favour the backward reaction; The hydrochloric acid will react with the precipitate of iron(III) hydroxide to form soluble iron(III) chloride and water.

d) Addition of $FeCl_3$ pushes the equilibrium to the right; forming more $Fe(OH)_3$

2. a) $2NO_2(g) \rightleftharpoons N_2O_4$ **(1 mark for correct formulae and $\rightleftharpoons$; 1 mark for balanced equation)**

b) the reaction is exothermic; cooling the mixture will cause the equilibrium to shift to the right, N_2O_4 is formed which is pale yellow; the reverse reaction is endothermic; heating the mixture shifts the equilibrium to the left

Pages 118–119 Energy Changes

Multiple-choice questions

1. D **2.** C **3.** B **4.** A

Short-answer questions

1. the burner must be weighed before; and after the fuel is burned

2. the temperature must be measured before and after the change

3. to minimise heat exchange with the air outside; to make the measurement of energy change as accurate as possible;

4. $1 cm^3$ of water has a mass of $1 g$ (density is $1 g/cm^3$); so volume in cm^3 = mass in g

5. each solution contributes $25 cm^3$ water, so $50 cm^3$ water is present; $50 cm^3$ = $50 g$;

GCSE-style questions

1. a) **(1 mark for points correctly plotted; 1 mark for line, which should go through all points apart from the last)**

b) **(circle around the result for pentanol)**

c) as the number of carbon atoms increases; the energy released increases

d) allow any value in the range 38–42 kJ/g; **(value should be taken from your graph)**

e) soot is solid carbon; produced by incomplete combustion of the fuel

Answer all parts of all questions. Continue on a separate sheet of paper if necessary.

1 Sam is a research scientist. He is asked to investigate an isotope of bromine that is found to be radioactive. Sam carries out an experiment where he places different materials between a sample of the bromine isotope and a detector.

a) Describe the results that you would expect Sam to get if the material was emitting both beta and gamma radiation. **(3 marks)**

....

....

....

b) Describe what safety precautions Sam should take when carrying out this experiment. **(2 marks)**

....

....

c) Sam reads that the radioactive decay of the bromine isotope has a 'half-life' of 2.4 hours. State what is meant by the term 'half-life'. **(1 mark)**

....

d) ✎ Sam is confused to find another book that says 'it is impossible to say how long it will be before any individual atom decays.' Explain how both the comments read by Sam can be true. **(6 marks)**

....

....

....

....

....

....

e) A colleague tells Sam that heating the bromine isotope will increase the rate of decay. Is this true or false? **(1 mark)**

....

Score   / 13

Physics

How well did you do?

| 0–8 | Try again | 9–14 | Getting there | 15–19 | Good work | 20–27 | Excellent! |

For more information on this topic, see pages 62–63 of your Success Revision Guide.

Living with Radioactivity

Multiple-choice questions

Choose just one answer: A, B, C or D.

1 Identify the correct statement. **(1 mark)**
- **A** all types of radiation are equally dangerous
- **B** the majority of background exposure to radiation is natural
- **C** gamma rays are the most energetic and therefore most ionising
- **D** alpha particles are the most massive and therefore most difficult to stop

2 A radioactive leak consists of a mixture of substances with different properties. Which of the following presents the greatest long-term problem? **(1 mark)**
- **A** high activity, short half-life, chemically inert
- **B** low activity, long half-life, chemically inert
- **C** low activity, long half-life, readily incorporated into biomolecules
- **D** high activity, short half-life, readily incorporated into biomolecules

3 Which of the following is the greatest source of background radiation? **(1 mark)**
- **A** rocks and buildings
- **B** nuclear power
- **C** food and drink
- **D** radon gas

4 Which of the following would block beta but not gamma radiation? **(1 mark)**
- **A** paper
- **B** 50 mm lead
- **C** clothing
- **D** 5 mm aluminium

5 People who fly frequently are at risk from increased exposure to what type of background radiation? **(1 mark)**
- **A** radon gas
- **B** cosmic rays
- **C** consumption of irradiated food
- **D** radioactive waste

Score   / 5

Short-answer questions

1 a) The following statements are true:
- One source of the background radiation exposure we receive is from our food.

- Modern food industry practice includes irradiation of some foods in order to increase their shelf-life. The conclusion that food irradiation contributes to our background exposure is, however, a misconception. Explain why. (2 marks)

b) Following the Chernobyl incident of 1986, grass used for grazing sheep in Britain was contaminated with radioactive material. To protect the public, these sheep were not used for food. Why are the consequences of contamination of the food chain of serious concern in terms of radiation exposure to our bodies? (2 marks)

Score   / 4

Answer all parts of all questions. Continue on a separate sheet of paper if necessary.

1 The following chart indicates the different sources of background radiation.

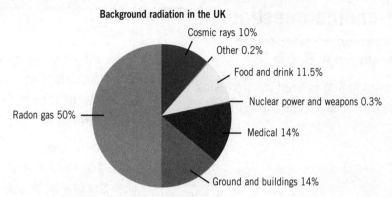

Background radiation in the UK

Cosmic rays 10%
Other 0.2%
Food and drink 11.5%
Nuclear power and weapons 0.3%
Medical 14%
Radon gas 50%
Ground and buildings 14%

a) Complete the sentence: 'Background radiation refers to...' **(1 mark)**

b) Given that radon is a gas that is itself radioactive, explain why special precautions are needed for buildings built upon granite. **(2 marks)**

c) ✐ The decay products of radon are not gases, but solids. Although external exposure to alpha radiation is not generally hazardous, what are the possible consequences for health of inhalation of radon? **(6 marks)**
(Answer on a separate sheet)

2 A scientist has a small spillage of a radioactive material in the laboratory. He uses a Geiger counter to monitor the area, obtaining a reading of 212 Bq. With a half-life of 110 min, she calculates that the activity will have decayed effectively to zero by the following day and so is surprised to find an activity of approximately 2 Bq when she checks the area.

a) Describe what calculation the scientist used to justify thinking that the material would have decayed within 24 hours. **(2 marks)**

b) Describe the basic experimental error that she made that accounts for the remaining count of 2 Bq. **(2 marks)**

Score / 13

How well did you do?

| 0–6 | Try again | 7–11 | Getting there | 12–16 | Good work | 17–22 | Excellent! |

For more information on this topic, see pages 64–65 of your Success Revision Guide.

Physics

Uses of Radioactive Materials

Multiple-choice questions

Choose just one answer: A, B, C or D.

1 What kind of radiation is used for sterilising medical equipment or increasing the shelf-life of food? **(1 mark)**
- **A** alpha
- **B** beta
- **C** gamma
- **D** X-ray

2 Radiation workers must avoid occupational exposure as much as possible. Which of the following is NOT a means of reducing exposure? **(1 mark)**
- **A** monitoring
- **B** reducing contact time
- **C** using shielding
- **D** maximising their distance

3 In which of the following processes is radioactivity NOT involved? **(1 mark)**
- **A** locating blockages in underground pipes
- **B** smoke detection
- **C** cancer treatment
- **D** laser printing

4 In igneous rocks, lead is a stable product formed by the decay of uranium radioisotopes. The ratio of lead to uranium can be used for dating. If the ratio is 3:1, how many half-lives have elapsed since the rock solidified? **(1 mark)**
- **A** 1
- **B** 2
- **C** 3
- **D** 4

5 Material that once was living can be dated using a radioisotope of which element? **(1 mark)**
- **A** oxygen
- **B** potassium
- **C** carbon
- **D** nitrogen

Score   / 5

Short-answer questions

1 The radioisotope americium-241 is used in smoke detectors.

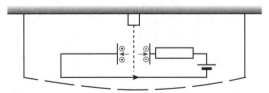

With reference to how the smoke alarm works, explain why beta and gamma radiation could not be used in the same way. **(2 marks)**

....

....

2 An underground pipe is suspected to have a leak somewhere in a 100 m stretch. A radioisotope tracer could be used to locate and patch the leak. State what type of emission is needed for this technique and explain your choice. **(2 marks)**

....

....

Score   / 4

Physics

64

Answer all parts of all questions. Continue on a separate sheet of paper if necessary.

1 Aluminium foil production can be monitored using a radioactive source and detector in order to standardise thickness, as shown in the diagram.

a) Describe how measuring the radioactivity passing through the foil be used to judge thickness. **(1 mark)**

b) State the type of emission that would be most appropriate. **(1 mark)**

c) State if your answer to **b)** would differ if the material being produced was sheet steel and explain your answer. **(2 marks)**

d) Would an isotope of long or short half-life be most advantageous for this type of industrial process? Explain your answer. **(2 marks)**

2 The radioisotope technetium-99 m, which is used for bone scans, decays by gamma emission with a half-life of 6 h. It is linked to a phosphate derivative and injected into the patient, where it gets incorporated at sites of bone growth. A camera can then be used to scan the patient for sites of accumulation – for example, to aid diagnosis of bone cancers. Explain, by referring to patient risk and patient benefit, why this technique would be justified to aid management of a cancer patient. **(2 marks)**

Score   / 8

How well did you do?

| 0–4 | Try again | 5–9 | Getting there | 10–13 | Good work | 14–17 | Excellent! |

Physics

For more information on this topic, see pages 66–67 of your Success Revision Guide.

Nuclear Fission and Fusion

Multiple-choice questions

Choose just one answer: A, B, C or D.

1 The energy-releasing process that occurs in stars is: **(1 mark)**
- **A** fission
- **B** fissile
- **C** fusion
- **D** futile

2 Which of the following statements is true regarding the renewability of nuclear power? **(1 mark)**
- **A** fusion is renewable but fission is not
- **B** fission is renewable but fusion is not
- **C** both fission and fusion are renewable
- **D** neither fission nor fusion are renewable

3 A self-sustaining series of fission events is called a: **(1 mark)**
- **A** domino effect
- **B** neutron shower
- **C** chain reaction
- **D** landslide reaction

4 In a fission reactor the purpose of the moderator is: **(1 mark)**
- **A** to prevent a chain reaction
- **B** to slow down the neutrons to encourage a chain reaction
- **C** to increase the energy output
- **D** to reduce radioactive waste products

5 A major environmental advantage of nuclear power is: **(1 mark)**
- **A** many jobs are created
- **B** no pollutant gases are released
- **C** the energy released per kg of fuel is very high
- **D** power stations require a plentiful water supply

Score   / 5

Short-answer questions

1 a) Fill in the missing words to complete these statements about nuclear reactors. **(6 marks)**

   i) The .... are made of uranium-235 or plutonium-239.

   ii) A .... is used to slow down the neutrons so that they can be absorbed.

   iii) The energy heats up the ....

   iv) A .... is circulated to remove the heat.

   v) The hot coolant is used to produce steam, which drives the power station's ....

   vi) Control rods can be moved into the reactor to absorb .... and slow or stop the reaction.

b) Draw lines to match the different levels of radioactive waste to the disposal method used. **(2 marks)**

Low level waste	Kept under water in cooling tanks
Intermediate level waste	Mixed with concrete and stored in stainless steel containers.
High level waste	Sealed into containers and put in landfill sites.

Score   / 8

Answer all parts of all questions. Continue on a separate sheet of paper if necessary.

1 The following nuclear equation describes the process of nuclear fusion, which occurs in stars. It is responsible for releasing large amounts of electromagnetic radiation.

$$^2_1H + {}^1_1H \longrightarrow {}^3_2He$$

a) State what type of force must be overcome in order to allow the nuclear strong force to take over and join the nuclei together.   **(1 mark)**

....

b) Scientists are working to try and create conditions that would allow fusion to occur as a means of generating electricity.

   i)   State the two extreme conditions that are needed, which scientists are struggling to achieve.   **(2 marks)**

   ....

   ....

   ii) State TWO advantages that this process has over the existing process of nuclear power generation.   **(2 marks)**

   ....

   ....

2 When U-235 undergoes fission two new nuclei are formed, such as Barium-141 and Krypton-92.

a) Complete the following decay equation: **(2 marks)**

$$^{235}_{92}U + {}^1_0n \longrightarrow {}^{\square}_{56}Ba + {}^{92}_{\square}Kr + 3\,{}^1_0n$$

b) An alternative pair of daughter nuclei is Xenon-140 (Z = 54) and Strontium-94 (Z = 38). Calculate how many neutrons are released by this fission event.   **(1 mark)**

....

c) Write a decay equation for the fission event in part **b)**.   **(3 marks)**

....

....

Score   / 11

How well did you do?

| 0–6 | Try again | 7–12 | Getting there | 13–18 | Good work | 19–24 | Excellent! |

For more information on this topic, see pages 68–69 of your Success Revision Guide.

67

Physics

Stars

Multiple-choice questions

Choose just one answer: A, B, C or D.

1 In which part of a star does thermonuclear fusion take place? **(1 mark)**
- **A** core
- **B** protostar
- **C** nucleus
- **D** nebula

2 Which gas is produced by the nuclear fusion of hydrogen? **(1 mark)**
- **A** oxygen
- **B** carbon dioxide
- **C** hydrogen oxide
- **D** helium

3 What is the explosion that occurs when a very massive star comes to an end? **(1 mark)**
- **A** big bang
- **B** supernova
- **C** white dwarf
- **D** red supergiant

4 What will our Sun become at the end of its 'life cycle'? **(1 mark)**
- **A** red giant
- **B** supernova
- **C** black dwarf
- **D** planetary nebula

5 Which is the second most common element in the Universe? **(1 mark)**
- **A** hydrogen
- **B** carbon
- **C** oxygen
- **D** helium

Score   / 5

Short-answer questions

1 a) State which force is responsible for the formation of stars. (1 mark)

....

b) Describe why stars do not keep contracting because of this force. (2 marks)

....

....

2 Label this diagram of the life cycle of a star that is more massive than our Sun. (5 marks)

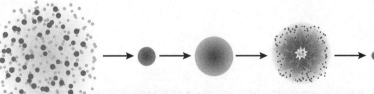

A   B   C   D   E

....

Score   / 8

Answer all parts of all questions. Continue on a separate sheet of paper if necessary.

1 After 10 000 million years the Sun is expected to run out of the hydrogen that fuels nuclear fusion.

a) ✐ Explain the stages involved when a star like the Sun comes towards the end of its 'life cycle'. **(6 marks)**

b) In contrast to the Sun, the star Rigel is expected to undergo a different fate. Rigel, in the constellation Orion, has a mass 17 times greater than that of the Sun. Describe how Rigel's fate will differ from that of the Sun. **(3 marks)**

2 Explain why the core of a star must be at a temperature of many millions of degrees Celsius. **(3 marks)**

3 In 1604, Kepler observed a supernova in the constellation Ophiuchus, within the Milky Way galaxy. It occurred at a distance of 20 000 light years.
Calculate the year in which the supernova actually happened. **(1 mark)**

Score   / 13

Physics

How well did you do?

| 0–6 | Try again | 7–12 | Getting there | 13–19 | Good work | 20–26 | Excellent! |

For more information on this topic, see pages 70–71 of your Success Revision Guide.

Atomic Structure

Multiple-choice questions

Choose just one answer: A, B, C or D.

1 Which particle found in an atom has no charge? **(1 mark)**
- **A** electron
- **B** neutron
- **C** nucleon
- **D** proton

2 What is the mass number of an atom? **(1 mark)**
- **A** number of neutrons
- **B** number of neutrons – number of electrons
- **C** number of neutrons + number of protons
- **D** number of protons

3 What do the two atoms $^{31}_{15}P$ and $^{32}_{16}S$ have in common? The same number of: **(1 mark)**
- **A** neutrons and protons
- **B** neutrons

- **C** protons and electrons
- **D** protons

4 What is the total number of protons in one molecule of water? **(1 mark)**
- **A** 9
- **B** 10
- **C** 17
- **D** 18

5 Isotopes of an element have different: **(1 mark)**
- **A** atomic numbers
- **B** numbers of electrons
- **C** numbers of neutrons
- **D** numbers of protons

Score   / 5

Short-answer questions

1 Complete the following passage.

All atoms are made up of a small dense nucleus. Surrounding the nucleus are ....

Most atoms contain three different particles: protons, ... and electrons.

.... are positively charged and have a relative mass of ....

.... are negatively charged and .... have no charge. All atoms of the same

element contain the same number of .... and .... Atoms of the same

element with a different number of .... are known as ....   **(10 marks)**

2 Deuterium $^{2}_{1}D$ and tritium $^{3}_{1}T$ are isotopes of hydrogen.

a) How many electrons are there in a deuterium atom? ....   **(1 mark)**

b) How many protons are there in a tritium atom? ....   **(1 mark)**

c) How does the nucleus of a tritium atom differ from the nucleus of a deuterium

atom? ....   **(1 mark)**

Score   / 13

Answer all parts of all questions. Continue on a separate sheet of paper if necessary.

❶ Complete the table below, which is about the three types of particle found in an atom. **(3 marks)**

	Relative mass	Relative charge	Where found in the atom
electron			
proton			
neutron			

❷ The diagram represents an atom of lithium (Li).

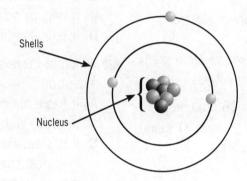

Shells

Nucleus

a) What is represented by each of the symbols? **(3 marks)**

   i) grey dot ....

   ii) red dot ....

   iii) green dot ....

b) What are shells? **(2 marks)**

....

....

c) Explain why lithium has a mass number of 7 and an atomic number of 3. **(2 marks)**

....

....

....

d) Write the symbol for lithium showing the mass number and atomic number. **(1 mark)**

....

Score   / 11

Chemistry

How well did you do?

| 0–7 | Try again | | 8–14 | Getting there | | 15–21 | Good work | | 22–29 | Excellent! |

For more information on this topic, see pages 74–75 of your Success Revision Guide.

Atoms and the Periodic Table

Multiple-choice questions

Choose just one answer: A, B, C or D.

1 Which of these is true about atoms of elements in the same period of the periodic table? **(1 mark)**
- **A** they have the same number of protons in the nucleus
- **B** they have the same number of electrons in their outer shells
- **C** they have the same number of electron shells
- **D** they all have the same atomic mass

2 If an atom of an element has 16 protons, it follows that: **(1 mark)**
- **A** the atom will have 16 electrons
- **B** the atomic mass of the atom must be 32
- **C** the atom will have 16 neutrons
- **D** the atom will have a full outer shell

3 Which particles are present in the nucleus of an atom? **(1 mark)**
- **A** protons, neutrons and electrons
- **B** neutrons and electrons
- **C** protons only
- **D** protons and neutrons

4 Which of these statements about the atomic number of an element is incorrect? **(1 mark)**
- **A** it tells us how many protons the atom has
- **B** it tells us how many electrons the atom has
- **C** it tells us how many neutrons the atom has
- **D** it tells us which element the atom is

5 Which of these statements correctly describes a neutron? **(1 mark)**
- **A** it has a mass of one amu and a negative charge
- **B** it has a mass of two amu and no electrical charge
- **C** it has a mass of one amu and a positive charge
- **D** it has a mass of one amu and no electrical charge

Score / 5

Short-answer questions

1 What is the link between the group number in the periodic table and the electron arrangement of an atom? (2 marks)

2 Lithium is in group 1, period 2. How are the electrons arranged in a lithium atom? (2 marks)

3 Explain why, despite containing electrically charged particles, an atom is neutral. (2 marks)

4 How many electrons can the second electron shell hold? (1 mark)

Score / 7

Answer all parts of all questions. Continue on a separate sheet of paper if necessary.

1 **a)** A carbon atom has atomic number 6 and mass number 12. How many neutrons

does it contain? .... **(1 mark)**

b) Where, in the carbon atom, are the neutrons found? .... **(1 mark)**

c) What information about a carbon atom can be deduced from the atomic number 6? **(2 marks)**

....

....

d) Mark, on the diagram, the arrangement of the electrons in the shells. **(2 marks)**

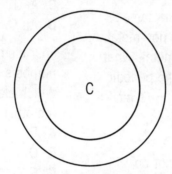

e) Where would the element carbon be placed in the periodic table? **(2 marks)**

....

f) Would you expect carbon to have metallic properties, non-metallic properties or
intermediate properties? Explain your answer. **(2 marks)**

....

....

....

2 Explain why the mass of the atom (amu) is the same as the number of protons added
to the number of neutrons in the nucleus. **(3 marks)**

....

....

....

Score   / 13

How well did you do?

| 0–6 | Try again | 7–12 | Getting there | 13–19 | Good work | 20–25 | Excellent! |

For more information on this topic, see pages 76–77 of your Success Revision Guide.

73

Chemistry

The Periodic Table

Chemistry

Multiple-choice questions

Choose just one answer: A, B, C or D.

1 The elements in the periodic table are placed in order of their increasing: **(1 mark)**
- **A** atomic mass
- **B** density
- **C** proton number
- **D** radius

2 X, Y and Z are three elements in the same period of the periodic table. X is a non-metal, Y is a metal and Z is a transition metal. What is the order of these elements in the periodic table? **(1 mark)**
- **A** X, Z, Y
- **B** Y, X, Z
- **C** Y, Z, X
- **D** Z, Y, X

3 Which property of an element cannot be predicted from its position in the periodic table? **(1 mark)**
- **A** electronic configuration
- **B** mass number
- **C** number of protons
- **D** number of isotopes

4 Gold (Au) is a transition metal. What is the formula of gold(I) oxide? **(1 mark)**
- **A** Au_2O
- **B** AuO
- **C** AuO_2
- **D** Au_2O_3

5 Four elements, P, Q, R and S, have proton numbers respectively of 2, 3, 5 and 10. Which element is not in the same period as the other three? **(1 mark)**
- **A** P
- **B** Q
- **C** R
- **D** S

Score / 5

Short-answer questions

1 The 'Law of Triads' grouped elements into threes, based on their properties. It was noted that, for a given property, the middle element in the triad had a value that was approximately the average of the values of the first and last elements.

a) Use the Law of Triads to complete the table. (2 marks)

Property	Sulfur	Selenium	Tellurium
relative atomic mass	32	79	
boiling point (°C)	445		987

b) Who proposed this law? (1 mark)

c) Name a physical property, other than melting point, that would obey this law. (1 mark)

d) Why was the Law of Triads dismissed as simply a 'curious coincidence' when it was first proposed?

(1 mark)

Score / 5

74

Answer all parts of all questions. Continue on a separate sheet of paper if necessary.

1 The diagram shows the top half of the periodic table. The letters are NOT the chemical symbols of the elements.

(16 marks)

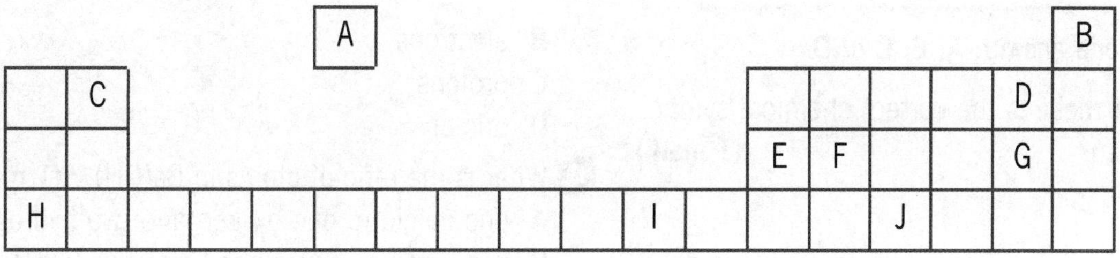

| | | | | | | | | | | | | | | | | | A | | | | | | | | | | | B |

(periodic table grid with letters: A, C, B, D, E, F, G, H, I, J)

Answer the questions using only these letters.

a) Which TWO elements are in the same group? ....

b) Which TWO elements are in the second period? ....

c) Which element has the electronic configuration 2, 8, 4? ....

d) Which is the most reactive non-metal? ....

e) Which is the most reactive metal? ....

f) Which element has THREE electrons in its outermost shell? ....

g) Which element is a noble gas? ....

h) Which element is in group 5? ....

i) Which element has the most protons? ....

j) Which element is a transition metal? ....

k) Which element appears to belong to no group? ....

l) Which TWO elements form ions that have the electronic structure 2, 8, 8? ....

m) Compare the electronic structures of elements D and G. How are they:

  i) similar ....

  ii) different? ....

n) Compare the electronic structures of elements E and G. How are they:

  i) similar ....

  ii) different? ....

Score   / 16

Chemistry

How well did you do?

| 0–6 | Try again | 7–13 | Getting there | 14–19 | Good work | 20–26 | Excellent! |

For more information on this topic, see pages 78–79 of your Success Revision Guide.

Chemical Reactions and Atoms

Multiple-choice questions

Choose just one answer: A, B, C or D.

1 Which of these is the correct chemical symbol for sodium? **(1 mark)**
- **A** S
- **B** So
- **C** N
- **D** Na

2 What is a 'cation'? **(1 mark)**
- **A** a metal atom that has lost one or more electrons
- **B** a metal atom that has gained one or more electrons
- **C** a non-metal atom that has gained one or more electrons
- **D** a non-metal atom with a negative charge

3 Which particles are involved when atoms bond together? **(1 mark)**
- **A** neutrons
- **B** electrons
- **C** protons
- **D** nuclei

4 What is the ratio of atoms in $Ca(OH)_2$? **(1 mark)**
- **A** one calcium, one oxygen and two hydrogen
- **B** two calcium, two oxygen and two hydrogen
- **C** one calcium, two oxygen and two hydrogen
- **D** two calcium, one oxygen and one hydrogen

5 The law of conservation of mass states that: **(1 mark)**
- **A** the mass of the reactants is always greater than the mass of the products
- **B** the mass of the products is always greater than the mass of the reactants
- **C** the mass of the products of a chemical reaction is always the same
- **D** the mass of the reactants is always the same as the mass of the products

Score / 5

Short-answer questions

1 Which elements are present in NH_4OH, and in what ratio? (2 marks)

2 Which type of bonding would you expect in copper oxide? Explain why. (2 marks)

3 Does 'CO' represent an element or a compound? Explain how you can tell. (2 marks)

4 What must sulfur trioxide, SO_3, react with to make sulfuric acid, H_2SO_4? (2 marks)

5 What has happened to a calcium atom if it has become a Ca^{2+} ion? (2 marks)

Score / 10

Answer all parts of all questions. Continue on a separate sheet of paper if necessary.

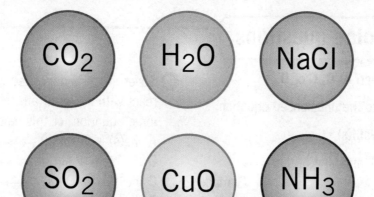

1 **a)** What do these six substances have in common? (2 marks)

....

....

b) In which of these substances would you expect atoms to be joined by ionic bonding?
Explain your choice. (2 marks)

....

....

c) Which two substances are 'dioxides'? How can you tell? (2 marks)

....

....

d) Give two reasons why the formula H_2O is more useful to a scientist than the
name 'water'. (2 marks)

....

....

e) What information is given by the formula NH_3? (2 marks)

....

....

Score   / 10

Chemistry

How well did you do?

| 0–6 | Try again | 7–12 | Getting there | 13–19 | Good work | 20–25 | Excellent! |

For more information on this topic, see pages 80–81 of your Success Revision Guide.

Balancing Equations

Multiple-choice questions

Choose just one answer: A, B, C or D.

Questions 1–3 refer to the unbalanced equation:

$$Na(s) + Cl_2(g) \longrightarrow NaCl(s)$$

1 What is the BEST meaning of the $\longrightarrow$ symbol? **(1 mark)**

   A is formed from
   B reacts to form
   C will become
   D will make

2 What do the symbols 's' and 'g' represent? **(1 mark)**

   A how reactive the chemicals are
   B the state symbols of the chemicals
   C the structure of the chemicals
   D the type of bonding in the chemicals

3 Which reaction is correctly balanced? **(1 mark)**

   A $2Na(s) + Cl_2(g) \longrightarrow 2NaCl(s)$
   B $2Na(s) + Cl_2(g) \longrightarrow Na_2Cl_2(s)$
   C $Na(s) + Cl(g) \longrightarrow NaCl(s)$
   D $Na(s) + Cl_2(g) \longrightarrow NaCl_2(s)$

4 Silver metal is deposited when iron filings react with silver nitrate solution. What is the ionic equation for this reaction? **(1 mark)**

   A $Fe(s) + 2Ag^+(aq) \longrightarrow Fe^{2+}(aq) + 2Ag(s)$
   B $Fe^{2+}(aq) + Ag^+(aq) \longrightarrow Fe^{3+}(aq) + Ag(s)$
   C $Fe^{3+}(aq) + 3Ag(s) \longrightarrow Fe(s) + 3Ag^+(aq)$
   D $Fe^{3+}(aq) + Ag(s) \longrightarrow Fe^{2+}(aq) + Ag^+(aq)$

5 Sulfur trioxide is manufactured by the reaction between sulfur dioxide and oxygen. The equation for the reaction is

$$xSO_2 + yO_2 \longrightarrow zSO_3$$

What are the values for x, y and z in the equation? **(1 mark)**

	x	y	z
A	1	1	1
B	1	2	2
C	2	1	2
D	2	2	1

Score   / 5

Short-answer questions

1 Balance the following equations. You will not have to write a number in every space. **(6 marks)**

a) .... $H_2(g) +$ .... $O_2(g) \longrightarrow$ .... $H_2O(l)$

b) .... $C(s) +$ .... $CO_2(g) \longrightarrow$ .... $CO(g)$

c) .... $Cl_2(g) +$ .... $KBr(aq) \longrightarrow$ .... $Br_2(l) +$ .... $KCl(aq)$

d) .... $N_2(g) +$ .... $H_2(g) \longrightarrow$ .... $NH_3(g)$

e) .... $CH_4(g) +$ .... $O_2(g) \longrightarrow$ .... $CO_2(g) +$ .... $H_2O(g)$

f) .... $CuO(s) +$ .... $NH_3(g) \longrightarrow$ .... $Cu(s) +$ .... $H_2O(l) +$ .... $N_2(g)$

Score   / 6

Answer all parts of all questions. Continue on a separate sheet of paper if necessary.

❶ Fill in the gaps by choosing from the following words. (6 marks)

elements   atoms   number   one   products   sides   state   three

There are four steps in writing a balanced chemical equation.

1. Write down the correct formulae of the reactants and ....

2. Check the number of .... of each element on both ....
of the equation.

3. Balance the equation by placing a .... in front of the formulae of

the substances in the equation. The number .... is not written.

4. Include the .... symbols in the equation.

❷ The chemical reaction for the respiration of glucose ($C_6H_{12}O_6$) is (2 marks)

$$C_6H_{12}O_6(s) + 6O_2(g) \longrightarrow 6CO_2(g) + 6H_2O(g)$$

a) Complete this sentence:
1 mole of glucose reacts with .... to give ....

....

b) i) What is the total number of carbon atoms, hydrogen atoms and oxygen atoms
on the left hand side of the equation? (1 mark)

carbon atoms: .... hydrogen atoms: ....

oxygen atoms: ....

ii) What is the total number of carbon atoms, hydrogen atoms and

oxygen atoms on the right hand side of the equation? (1 mark)

carbon atoms: .... hydrogen atoms: ....

oxygen atoms: ....

c) State, giving a reason, whether or not the equation is balanced. (2 marks)

....

....

....

Score   / 12

Chemistry

How well did you do?

| 0–5 | Try again | 6–11 | Getting there | 12–17 | Good work | 18–23 | Excellent! |

For more information on this topic, see pages 82–83 of your Success Revision Guide.

Ionic and Covalent Bonding

Multiple-choice questions

Choose just one answer: A, B, C or D.

1 What name is given to a charged particle? **(1 mark)**
- **A** atom
- **B** ion
- **C** ionic
- **D** molecule

2 Which pair of elements is most likely to form a covalent compound? **(1 mark)**
- **A** calcium and oxygen
- **B** magnesium and oxygen
- **C** magnesium and sulfur
- **D** sulfur and oxygen

3 Compound X is made up of chlorine and one other element. Which property shows that X is an ionic compound? **(1 mark)**
- **A** it conducts electricity when molten
- **B** it does NOT conduct electricity when solid

- **C** it is a solid at room temperature
- **D** it is insoluble in water

4 Which substance has the electronic structure shown in the diagram? **(1 mark)**

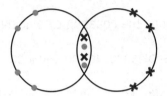

- **A** hydrogen (H_2)
- **B** hydrogen chloride (HCl)
- **C** oxygen (O_2)
- **D** sodium chloride (NaCl)

5 How many electrons are transferred when magnesium reacts with oxygen to form the ionic compound MgO? **(1 mark)**
- **A** 1 **B** 2 **C** 3 **D** 4

Score / 5

Short-answer questions

1 The diagram shows the arrangement of electrons in a molecule of methane (CH_4).

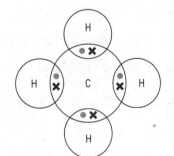

a) How many: **(4 marks)**

i) electrons are there in an atom of hydrogen ....

ii) electrons are there in an atom of carbon ....

iii) covalent bonds are there in a molecule of methane ....

iv) shared pairs of electrons are there in a molecule of methane? ....

b) Lithium contains 3 electrons and fluorine contains 9 electrons. On a separate sheet of paper, draw a diagram to show the arrangement of electrons and the type of bonding in lithium fluoride. **(3 marks)**

Score / 7

Answer all parts of all questions. Continue on a separate sheet of paper if necessary.

1 The diagram shows the arrangement of electrons in a compound, P.

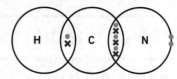

(3 marks)

   a) Name the elements present in compound P.

   b) How many single covalent bonds can be formed by: **(3 marks)**

      i) hydrogen ....

      ii) carbon ....

      iii) nitrogen? ....

   c) The bonds between carbon and nitrogen are not single covalent bonds. Suggest how they might be described. **(1 mark)**

2 Element Y reacts with chlorine to form an ionic compound, YCl_2.

   a) i) What would be the physical state of YCl_2 at room temperature? Give a reason for your answer. **(1 mark)**

      ii) Give TWO other properties of YCl_2. **(2 marks)**

   b) Is Y a metal or a non-metal? Give a reason for your answer. **(1 mark)**

   c) i) What is the charge on ion Y in the compound YCl_2? .... **(1 mark)**

      ii) Y reacts with oxygen to form an oxide. Deduce the formula of the oxide. **(1 mark)**

   d) Chlorine can also form covalent bonds. On a separate piece of paper, draw a dot-and-cross diagram of a covalent molecule of chlorine, Cl_2. **(3 marks)**

Score   / 16

How well did you do?

| 0–7 | Try again | 8–14 | Getting there | 15–21 | Good work | 22–28 | Excellent! |

For more information on this topic, see pages 84–85 of your Success Revision Guide.

Chemistry

Ionic and Covalent Structures

Multiple-choice questions

Choose just one answer: A, B, C or D.

Use the table to answer questions 1–3.

Substance	Particles	Structure	Forces
W	atoms	three-dimensional giant structure	strong
X	atoms	atoms arranged in planes	strong between atoms in planes; weak between planes
Y	atoms	molecular	strong between atoms in molecules; weak between molecules
Z	ions	three-dimensional giant structure	strong

1 Which substance could be
  sodium chloride? **(1 mark)**
  A W **B** X **C** Y **D** Z

2 Which substance could be graphite? **(1 mark)**
  A W **B** X **C** Y **D** Z

3 Which substance could be iodine? **(1 mark)**
  A W **B** X **C** Y **D** Z

4 Which substance has a giant atomic structure
  and conducts electricity? **(1 mark)**
  A diamond **B** graphite
  C silicon dioxide **D** sodium chloride

5 Which substance has a giant
  ionic structure? **(1 mark)**
  A diamond **B** graphite
  C silicon dioxide **D** sodium chloride

Score / 5

Short-answer questions

calcium carbonate   carbon dioxide   diamond   methane
neon   potassium chloride

1 From the above list of substances choose: (6 marks)

  a) two ionic compounds ....

  b) a substance that exists as individual atoms ....

  c) two compounds with weak forces between their particles ....

  d) two substances that exist as molecules ....

  e) a substance that exists as a giant covalent structure ....

  f) a compound that conducts electricity when molten ....

Score / 6

Answer all parts of all questions. Continue on a separate sheet of paper if necessary.

1 a) Silicon is an element immediately below carbon in group 4 of the periodic table.

How many electrons are there in the outer shell of silicon? _____ **(1 mark)**

b) Silicon is made by heating silicon dioxide with magnesium.

Write the word equation and a balanced symbol equation, including state symbols, for the reaction between magnesium and silicon dioxide. **(2 marks)**

....

....

c) i) Draw diagrams of magnesium and oxide ions and of the carbon dioxide molecules. **(4 marks)**

ii) Magnesium oxide and carbon dioxide can be made by burning the element in oxygen. Write a balanced symbol equation for each reaction. **(2 marks)**

....

....

iii) How does the structure of carbon dioxide differ from the structure of magnesium oxide? **(2 marks)**

....

....

d) Carbon dioxide is a gas at room temperature, whilst magnesium oxide is a solid.

Explain why magnesium oxide has a much higher melting point than carbon dioxide. **(3 marks)**

....

....

e) Under what conditions would magnesium oxide conduct electricity? **(1 mark)**

....

....

Score   / 15

Chemistry

How well did you do?

| 0–6 | Try again | 7–12 | Getting there | 13–19 | Good work | 20–26 | Excellent! |

For more information on this topic, see pages 86–87 of your Success Revision Guide.

Group 7

Multiple-choice questions

Choose just one answer: A, B, C or D.

1 Which halogen is a liquid at room temperature and pressure? **(1 mark)**
A bromine
B chlorine
C fluorine
D iodine

2 The element astatine (At) is immediately below iodine in group 7 of the periodic table. What is likely to be a property of astatine? **(1 mark)**
A it will be a liquid
B it will conduct electricity
C it will displace iodine from potassium iodide solution
D it will form a hydride, HAt

3 Which statement is correct about the ions of group 7 elements? **(1 mark)**
A each contains more protons than neutrons

B each contains more protons than electrons
C each has 7 electrons in its outermost shell
D each has a noble gas structure

4 What happens to the properties of the halogens as you go down group 7? **(1 mark)**
A the total number of valence electrons decreases
B their boiling points increase
C the forces between the molecules decrease
D they get more reactive

5 A new element, R, has 7 electrons in its outermost shell. Which statement about R is most likely to be correct? **(1 mark)**
A it will be diatomic
B it will form a positive ion, R^+
C it will form covalent compounds with group 1 elements
D it will have weak forces between its atoms

Score   / 5

Short-answer questions

1 Three experiments were performed in which a halogen, X_2, Y_2 or Z_2, was added to an aqueous solution containing ions of the other two halides.

The table shows the results of these experiments.

Experiment number	Halogen added	Solution contains halides ions of		
		X	Y	Z
1	X_2		Y_2 displaced	no reaction
2	Y_2	no reaction		no reaction
3	Z_2	X_2 displaced	Y_2 displaced	

Identify which halogen is chlorine, which is bromine and which is iodine. **(2 marks)**

X_2 is: .... Y_2 is: .... Z_2 is: ....

Score   / 2

Answer all parts of all questions. **Continue on a separate sheet of paper if necessary.**

1 The table gives some of the properties of fluorine, chlorine, bromine and iodine.

a) Complete the table by predicting the missing answers. pm is picometre (10^{-12} metres) **(6 marks)**

Halogen	Symbol	Electronic structure	Melting point °C	Boiling point °C	Atomic radius (pm)
	F	2, 7	−220	−188	
chlorine	Cl		−101	−35	99
bromine	Br	2, 8, 18, 7		59	114
iodine		2, 8, 18, 18, 7	114		144

b) Which halogen is a liquid at room temperature and pressure? Explain your answer. **(2 marks)**

c) Which molecule will have the greatest attraction between its molecules? Explain your answer. **(2 marks)**

d) From the table, predict which period of the periodic table bromine is in. Explain your answer. **(2 marks)**

2 Six atoms of a new halogen (UUS) were formed in 2010. The atom has a mass number of 294 and an atomic number of 117.

a) What is the number of each of the following particles in one atom of UUS? **(3 marks)**

  i) protons .... ii) neutrons .... iii) electrons ....

b) What is the relative molecular mass of UUS? .... **(1 mark)**

c) How many valence electrons are there in one atom of UUS? .... **(1 mark)**

d) What is the charge on the ion of UUS? .... **(1 mark)**

e) Predict the physical state of UUS. .... **(1 mark)**

f) Predict the reaction, if any, with an aqueous solution of potassium iodide. **(1 mark)**

Score   / 20

Chemistry

How well did you do?

| 0–6 | Try again | 7–12 | Getting there | 13–19 | Good work | 20–27 | Excellent! |

For more information on this topic, see pages 88–89 of your Success Revision Guide.

New Chemicals and Materials

Multiple-choice questions

Choose just one answer: A, B, C or D.

1 Which of these answers best describes nanoparticles? **(1 mark)**
- **A** naturally-occurring particles
- **B** very small particles
- **C** very large particles
- **D** very reactive particles

2 What do we call a manufacturing process that operates without interruption? **(1 mark)**
- **A** a batch process
- **B** a production line
- **C** a chemical synthesis
- **D** a continuous process

3 What is the chemical formula for buckminster fullerene? **(1 mark)**

- **A** C_{60}
- **B** $C_{30}H_{60}$
- **C** C_{30}
- **D** BF_{60}

4 Which of these is not an allotrope of carbon? **(1 mark)**
- **A** graphite
- **B** diamond
- **C** charcoal
- **D** buckminster fullerene

5 Which metallic element, when administered as nanoparticles, kills bacteria? **(1 mark)**
- **A** silver
- **B** calcium
- **C** magnesium
- **D** lithium

Score   / 5

Short-answer questions

1 State two chemicals that are manufactured in bulk by continuous process. (2 marks)

2 Why are many medicines produced in batch processes, rather than continuous processes? (2 marks)

3 Nanoparticles are so small that they can be absorbed directly through human skin. Why might working with nanoparticles be dangerous? (2 marks)

4 What holds the atoms together in fullerenes? (2 marks)

5 Briefly describe the structure of buckminster fullerenes. (2 marks)

Score   / 10

Answer all parts of all questions. Continue on a separate sheet of paper if necessary.

1 'Self-cleaning glass' is made by coating the glass with a layer of titanium oxide nanoparticles. The layer is so thin that it is completely transparent. The titanium oxide particles absorb light energy from the Sun and have a 'photocatalytic effect' on the breakdown of dirt and grime. The molecules of the dirt and grime are broken down and rinsed off with rainwater, so the glass remains clean.

a) Why would it be an advantage to use self-cleaning glass for windows in very tall tower-blocks? **(2 marks)**

b) Give two reasons why the titanium oxide layer should be as thin as possible. **(2 marks)**

c) What do you understand by the term 'photocatalytic effect'? **(2 marks)**

d) Why wouldn't builders of ordinary houses fit self-cleaning glass as standard? **(2 marks)**

e) Titanium oxide absorbs ultraviolet light. Why might this have benefits other than keeping the windows clean? **(2 marks)**

Chemistry

Score   / 10

How well did you do?

| 0–6 | Try again | 7–12 | Getting there | 13–19 | Good work | 20–25 | Excellent! |

For more information on this topic, see pages 90–91 of your Success Revision Guide.

Plastics and Perfumes

Multiple-choice questions

Choose just one answer: A, B, C or D.

1 What is a 'polymer'? (1 mark)

  A a hydrocarbon
  B a chain of monomers joined together
  C a thermoplastic material
  D a non-biodegradable material

2 Which of these polymers is the non-stick coating on pans? (1 mark)

  A PVC
  B polystyrene
  C polythene
  D PTFE

3 If polymer chains are cross-linked, the polymer will: (1 mark)

  A be a thermosetting material
  B have a lower melting point
  C be very flexible
  D be easier to mould and reshape

4 When a carboxylic acid and an alcohol react, what is produced? (1 mark)

  A a perfume
  B a solution
  C an unpleasant smell
  D an ester

5 Which of these is NOT responsible for the properties of a polymer? (1 mark)

  A the type of monomer
  B the length of the polymer chains
  C the degree of cross-linking
  D the cost of manufacture

Score   / 5

Short-answer questions

1 Name TWO natural polymers. (2 marks)

2 Name one man-made polymer and the monomer it is made from. (2 marks)

3 How does crystallinity affect the properties of a plastic? (2 marks)

4 What properties of PTFE make it suitable for coating frying pans? (2 marks)

5 Why should a perfume be volatile? (2 marks)

Score   / 10

Answer all parts of all questions. Continue on a separate sheet of paper if necessary.

1 Many household objects are made from polythene. A softened polythene sheet may be vacuum-formed into a shape, staying in that shape when the polythene cools. Polythene can have colouring pigments added to it to make brightly-coloured objects.

a) How is polythene made? **(2 marks)**

....

....

b) Polythene arrives at the factory as sacks of tiny granules. What has to be done to these granules to make the soft polythene sheet, ready for vacuum-forming? **(1 mark)**

....

c) Is polythene a thermoset or a thermoplastic material? Explain how you can tell. **(2 marks)**

....

....

....

d) Suggest what the advantages are of making a bucket out of polythene over the more traditional iron. **(2 marks)**

....

....

....

....

e) A polythene bucket has some plasticiser added to the polymer to make it less rigid. Why might this be necessary? **(2 marks)**

....

....

....

....

Score   / 9

Chemistry

How well did you do?

| 0–6 | Try again | 7–12 | Getting there | 13–18 | Good work | 19–24 | Excellent! |

For more information on this topic, see pages 92–93 of your Success Revision Guide.

Analysis

Multiple-choice questions

Choose just one answer: A, B, C or D.

1 What could paper chromatography be used to do? **(1 mark)**
- **A** identify the types of bond present in a molecule
- **B** see which food colourings have been used
- **C** check the amount of a pollutant in water
- **D** test for banned substances in blood

2 What technique is used to identify organic compounds with low boiling points? **(1 mark)**
- **A** thin-layer chromatography
- **B** gas chromatography
- **C** mass spectrometry
- **D** titration

3 In paper chromatography, what are substances identified by? **(1 mark)**
- **A** relative molecular mass
- **B** retention time
- **C** absorption wave number
- **D** R_f value

4 Which technique could reveal the relative molecular mass of a compound? **(1 mark)**
- **A** mass spectrometry
- **B** thin-layer chromatography
- **C** infra-red spectroscopy
- **D** gas chromatography

5 Which two techniques are often paired together in analysis? **(1 mark)**
- **A** paper chromatography and mass spectrometry
- **B** thin-layer chromatography and paper chromatography
- **C** gas chromatography and mass spectrometry
- **D** thin-layer chromatography and infra-red spectroscopy

Score / 5

Short-answer questions

1 What is the difference between qualitative analysis and quantitative analysis? (2 marks)

2 How is the R_f value of a spot on a chromatogram calculated? (2 marks)

3 Why might solvents other than water be necessary in chromatography? (2 marks)

4 Describe what is meant by the term 'retention time' in gas chromatography. (1 mark)

Score / 7

Answer all parts of all questions. Continue on a separate sheet of paper if necessary.

1 All Olympic athletes can expect to be routinely tested to ensure that they are not guilty of taking performance-enhancing drugs. Within a short time of the competition ending, the athletes are required to produce a sample of urine, which is sent to a laboratory for testing. In some cases, where prohibited substances have been identified, athletes have been disqualified from a competition and banned from competing in future events.

a) Why is the sample taken from the athlete very soon after they have competed?   **(2 marks)**

_____

_____

b) Why is it important that the sample is in a sealed container, with a barcode that identifies whose sample it is?   **(2 marks)**

_____

_____

c) i) Give an example of a combined analytical technique that could be used to identify the substances present in the athlete's urine sample.   **(1 mark)**

_____

   ii) Explain how the different substances are separated using this technique.   **(2 marks)**

_____

_____

_____

d) Why might a prohibited substance that had been taken not show up on the trace?   **(1 mark)**

_____

_____

e) Explain why it is possible to catch more of the athletes who cheat today than it was 50 years ago.   **(2 marks)**

_____

_____

_____

Score   / 10

Chemistry

How well did you do?

| 0–5 | Try again | 6–11 | Getting there | 12–17 | Good work | 18–22 | Excellent! |

For more information on this topic, see pages 94–95 of your Success Revision Guide.

Metals

Multiple-choice questions

Choose just one answer: A, B, C or D.

1 Which of these properties arise from metals having free electrons? **(1 mark)**
- **A** metals conduct electricity very well
- **B** metals can be hammered into shape
- **C** metals can be mixed to make alloys
- **D** metals are shiny when polished

2 Nitinol is a remarkable new metal because: **(1 mark)**
- **A** it is an alloy of nickel and titanium
- **B** it is particularly strong
- **C** it has an unusually low density
- **D** it regains its shape when heated

3 A metal can be a superconductor when: **(1 mark)**
- **A** heated to extremely high temperatures
- **B** cooled to very low temperatures
- **C** its electrical resistance is very high
- **D** wires can be made in very low diameters

4 Which of these properties is characteristic of non-metals? **(1 mark)**
- **A** very low electrical resistance
- **B** very high strength
- **C** ductility
- **D** low thermal conductivity

5 Metallic bonding arises from: **(1 mark)**
- **A** shared pairs of electrons
- **B** electron transfer from one atom to another
- **C** electrostatic attraction between ions and electrons
- **D** electrostatic attraction between oppositely charged ions

Score / 5

Short-answer questions

1 What type of structure do metals have? **(1 mark)**

2 Why do most metals have high melting points? **(2 marks)**

3 Why do metals become inefficient at conducting electricity when they become warmer? **(2 marks)**

4 What term describes an alloy that changes shape when it is heated? **(1 mark)**

5 What do you understand by the term 'delocalised electrons'? **(2 marks)**

6 Explain how delocalised electrons allow a metal to conduct electricity. **(2 marks)**

Score / 10

Answer all parts of all questions. Continue on a separate sheet of paper if necessary.

1 Gold is a very expensive metal because of its rarity. It is used for jewellery because it is very unreactive and it does not tarnish. Gold is often alloyed with copper and the purity of the gold is measured in 'carats'. 24-carat gold is pure gold.

a) Draw two pictures, one for 24-carat gold and one for 9-carat gold, showing the arrangement of the metal atoms. **(2 marks)**

b) Which would be more expensive – a ring made from 24-carat gold or a ring of the same size made from 9-carat gold? Explain why. **(2 marks)**

....

....

c) Which ring would be stronger? Explain why. **(2 marks)**

....

....

d) Suggest how a jeweller would be able to tell which ring was which, without damaging the rings. **(2 marks)**

....

....

e) Why should rings with different gold carat ratings never be worn together on the same finger? **(2 marks)**

....

....

Chemistry

Score / 10

How well did you do?

| 0–6 | Try again | 7–12 | Getting there | 13–18 | Good work | 19–25 | Excellent! |

For more information on this topic, see pages 96–97 of your Success Revision Guide.

Group 1

Multiple-choice questions

Choose just one answer: A, B, C or D.

1 Which element is NOT an alkali metal? **(1 mark)**
- **A** lithium
- **B** magnesium
- **C** potassium
- **D** sodium

2 Caesium is a group 1 element. What is the formula of caesium chloride? **(1 mark)**
- **A** CsCl
- **B** $CsCl_2$
- **C** Cs_2Cl
- **D** Cs_2Cl_3

3 Rubidium is below potassium in the periodic table. Which statement about rubidium is likely to be true? **(1 mark)**
- **A** rubidium hydroxide will be insoluble in water
- **B** it will be produced at the cathode when a solution of rubidium hydroxide is electrolysed
- **C** the formula of rubidium sulfate will be Rb_2SO_4
- **D** the melting point of rubidium will be higher than the melting point of potassium

4 Which equation correctly shows the symbol equation for the reaction between sodium and water? **(1 mark)**
- **A** $2Na(s) + H_2O(l) \longrightarrow Na_2O(aq) + H_2(g)$
- **B** $2Na(s) + 2H_2O(l) \longrightarrow 2NaOH(aq) + H_2(g)$
- **C** $Na(s) + 2H_2O(aq) \longrightarrow NaO_2(aq) + 2H_2(g)$
- **D** $Na(s) + H_2O(l) \longrightarrow NaOH(aq) + H(g)$

5 Which statement is true about group 1 elements? **(1 mark)**
- **A** their density decreases going down the group
- **B** they are soft with high melting points
- **C** they do not conduct electricity
- **D** they form ions with a charge of 1+

Score / 5

Short-answer questions

1 The table below gives some properties of metals in group 1 of the periodic table. pm is picometre (10^{-12} metres).

Alkali metal	Electronic structure	Melting point (°C)	Atomic radius (pm)
lithium		180	123
sodium	2, 8, 1		
potassium	2, 8, 8, 1		

a) i) What is the electronic structure for lithium? _____ **(1 mark)**

ii) Would the melting point of sodium be higher or lower than 180°C? _____ **(1 mark)**

iii) Would the atomic radius of potassium be larger or smaller than 123pm? _____ **(1 mark)**

b) Why do these metals have similar properties? **(1 mark)**

c) How many protons are there in an atom of potassium? _____ **(1 mark)**

Score / 5

Answer all parts of all questions. Continue on a separate sheet of paper if necessary.

1 Lithium is in group 1 of the periodic table. It is the element at the top of the group.

a) Would you expect lithium to be more reactive or less reactive than sodium? **(1 mark)**

b) Lithium is a reactive metal that burns in air.

i) What compound is formed when lithium burns in air? **(1 mark)**

ii) What compound is formed when lithium reacts with chlorine? **(1 mark)**

c) Lithium reacts with cold water to form lithium hydroxide and a gas.

i) Name the gas given off in this reaction. **(1 mark)**

ii) How would you show that a solution of lithium hydroxide was alkaline? **(1 mark)**

iii) Write the word equation for the reaction between lithium and water. **(2 marks)**

d) i) What is the formula of a lithium ion? **(1 mark)**

ii) How does a lithium ion differ from a lithium atom? **(2 marks)**

iii) Write an equation to show the formation of a lithium ion. **(2 marks)**

e) ✎ Explain what properties you would predict for the compound lithium fluoride. **(6 marks)**

Score / 18

How well did you do?

| 0–6 Try again | 7–12 Getting there | 13–20 Good work | 21–28 Excellent! |

Chemistry

For more information on this topic, see pages 98–99 of your Success Revision Guide.

Aluminium and Transition Metals

Multiple-choice questions

Choose just one answer: A, B, C or D.

1 What is the main ore of aluminium?　**(1 mark)**
  A bauxite　　　**B** clay
  C cryolite　　　**D** haematite

2 Which reaction takes place in the manufacture of aluminium?　**(1 mark)**
  A aluminium ions accept electrons to form aluminium atoms
  B aluminium oxide is decomposed by heat
  C aluminium oxide is reduced by carbon
  D aluminium reacts with the graphite electrodes

3 Which statement is true about both group 1 metals and transition metals?　**(1 mark)**
  A they are good catalysts
  B they are good conductors of electricity
  C they are reactive metals
  D they have low melting points

4 Which statement about the transition metals is NOT true?　**(1 mark)**
  A they are in period 3 of the periodic table
  B they form coloured compounds
  C they have higher melting points than group 1 metals
  D they occur between group 2 and group 3 in the periodic table

5 The chemical symbol for copper is:　**(1 mark)**
  A Co
  B Cp
  C Cr
  D Cu

Score　/ 5

Short-answer questions

1 The diagram shows an experiment to show how copper can be purified.

  a) Copper is deposited on the cathode. What does this tell you about the charge on the copper ion?　(1 mark)

  ....

  ....

  ....

  ....

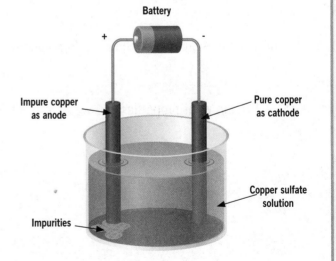

  b) Explain, with reasons, what happens to the blue colour of the copper(II) sulfate solution.

  (3 marks)

  ....

  ....

  ....

Score　/ 4

Answer all parts of all questions. Continue on a separate sheet of paper if necessary.

1 The diagram shows how aluminium is extracted from its ore by electrolysis.

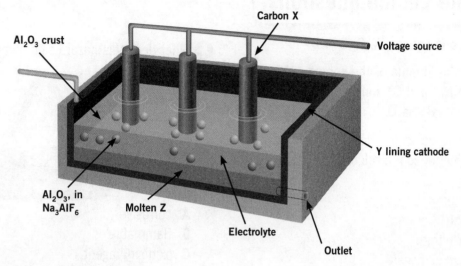

a) What is meant by 'electrolysis'? (2 marks)

....

b) Give the formulae of TWO of the ions present in the electrolyte.

....   (2 marks)

c) The word equation for the reaction taking place in the cell is:

aluminium oxide ⟶ aluminium + oxygen

Use this equation to explain the meaning of 'reduction'. (2 marks)

....

....

d) Explain why the following help to make the extraction process economical:

i) the building of a hydroelectric power (HEP) station to supply the plant with electricity (1 mark)

....

ii) the presence of a crust of aluminium oxide on the molten electrolyte. (1 mark)

....

....

Score   / 8

Chemistry

How well did you do?

| 0–5 | Try again | | 6–9 | Getting there | | 10–13 | Good work | | 14–17 | Excellent! |

For more information on this topic, see pages 100–101 of your Success Revision Guide.

Chemical Tests

Multiple-choice questions

Choose just one answer: A, B, C or D

1 What is the formula of the compound formed between Na^+ and O^{2-} ions? **(1 mark)**

A Na_2O **B** Na_2O_2 **C** NaO **D** NaO_2

2 What could be used to test for the presence of the chloride ion in dilute hydrochloric acid? **(1 mark)**

A bromine water
B copper(II) oxide
C silver nitrate
D sodium carbonate

3 Which gives a blue/green colour in a flame test? **(1 mark)**

A barium
B calcium
C copper
D sodium

4 What does this hazard sign mean? **(1 mark)**

A corrosive
B flammable
C oxidising agent
D toxic

5 What colour flame do calcium ions produce in a flame test? **(1 mark)**

A yellow
B red
C lilac
D green

Score / 5

Short-answer questions

1 Connect each metal to its correct flame colour. (4 marks)

barium	red
calcium	light green
lithium	crimson
sodium	yellow

2 A substance, G, was dissolved in water. Dilute nitric acid was added to the solution of G, followed by silver nitrate solution. A cream coloured precipitate, H, was formed.

a) What was precipitate H? (1 mark)

....

b) What negative ion was present in G? (1 mark)

....

Score / 6

Answer all parts of all questions. Continue on a separate sheet of paper if necessary.

1 Dave was given a white solid by his teacher. He was told that it was a salt and asked to identify it.

a) i) Dave started his analysis by carrying out a flame test. Describe the different stages of this test.   **(3 marks)**

....

....

....

....

ii) Give two safety precautions that Dave should take when carrying out the flame test.   **(2 marks)**

....

....

iii) Dave found that the salt produced a lilac flame. What does this tell him?   **(2 marks)**

....

b) Dave took some of the salt and dissolved it in water. He added some nitric acid and then a few drops of silver nitrate solution.

i) State what Dave was testing for.   **(1 mark)**

....

ii) If Dave's test proved negative, name three types of compound that could be ruled out.   **(3 marks)**

....

....

c) Dave added some barium chloride to his salt solution and a white precipitate was immediately formed.

What is the identity of the salt he has been given?   **(1 mark)**

....

Chemistry

Score   / 12

How well did you do?

| 0–6 | Try again | 7–12 | Getting there | 13–18 | Good work | 19–23 | Excellent! |

For more information on this topic, see pages 102–103 of your Success Revision Guide.

Acids and Bases

Multiple-choice questions

Choose just one answer: A, B, C or D.

1 Which pair of words describes the properties of sulfuric acid solution? **(1 mark)**

A strong aqueous
B strong solid
C weak aqueous
D weak solid

2 Which statement is true of acids in aqueous solution? **(1 mark)**

A they have a pH greater than 7
B they react with ammonium salts to give ammonia
C they react with any metal to give hydrogen
D they react with carbonates to give carbon dioxide

3 Which compound is a soluble base? **(1 mark)**

A aluminium oxide
B copper(II) oxide

C iron(III) hydroxide
D sodium hydroxide

4 Emma is suffering from an excess of acid in her stomach but she has no indigestion tablets. Which substance could Emma take to lower the acidity? **(1 mark)**

A common salt (pH 7)
B vinegar (pH 4)
C bicarbonate of soda (pH 8)
D lemon juice (pH 6)

5 Which substance reacts with dilute hydrochloric acid to give a gas and water as two of the three products? **(1 mark)**

A magnesium carbonate
B magnesium hydroxide
C magnesium oxide
D magnesium

Score / 5

Short-answer questions

1 Put a tick (✓) in the correct column to show whether a statement is true or false. (7 marks)

Statement	True	False
a) All acids release H^+ ions in water		
b) All acids contain oxygen		
c) All acids have a pH greater than 7		
d) All alkalis release OH^- ions in water		
e) Blue litmus paper turns red in alkaline solutions		
f) All metal oxides are alkalis		
g) Aqueous solutions of acids and alkalis contain ions		

Score / 7

Answer all parts of all questions. Continue on a separate sheet of paper if necessary.

1 Hydrochloric acid is a strong acid and ethanoic acid is a weak acid.

a) Complete the following equations by inserting the correct symbol to show that **(2 marks)**

  i) hydrochloric acid is a strong acid

  ii) ethanoic acid is a weak acid.

$$HCl(aq) \text{.............} H^+(aq) + Cl^-(aq)$$

$$CH_3COOH(aq) \text{.............} CH_3COO^-(aq) + H^+(aq)$$

b) Complete the following table to compare the properties of hydrochloric acid and ethanoic acid. **(3 marks)**

Reaction	Hydrochloric acid	Ethanoic acid
A – with magnesium	fast reaction	
B – with sodium carbonate and excess acid		carbon dioxide given off
C – pH	1	

c) i) What is meant by 'excess'? **(1 mark)**

  ii) In reaction B in the table above, will more, less or the same volume of gas be given off in both reactions when added in excess to the same mass of sodium carbonate. Explain your answer. **(2 marks)**

d) Which of these acids:

  i) is produced in the stomach **(1 mark)**

  ii) is present in vinegar? **(1 mark)**

2 Ammonia is a weak alkali.

a) Give the name of a strong alkali. **(1 mark)**

b) i) Give TWO uses of a strong alkali. **(2 marks)**

  ii) Give ONE use of ammonia. **(1 mark)**

Score   / 14

How well did you do?

| 0–6 | Try again | 7–13 | Getting there | 14–19 | Good work | 20–26 | Excellent! |

For more information on this topic, see pages 104–105 of your Success Revision Guide.

Chemistry

Making Salts

Multiple-choice questions

Choose just one answer: A, B, C or D.

1 A reaction between an acid and an alkali: **(1 mark)**
- **A** produces only water
- **B** always produces a salt
- **C** always produces hydrogen
- **D** always requires energy

2 The salt produced by reacting copper oxide and sulfuric acid is: **(1 mark)**
- **A** copper sulfate
- **B** sulfur dioxide
- **C** copper sulfide
- **D** copper sulfite

3 The pH of a dilute solution of ammonia in water would be: **(1 mark)**
- **A** between 1 and 3
- **B** between 4 and 6
- **C** between 8 and 11
- **D** between 12 and 14

4 Mixing barium chloride and sodium sulfate solutions produces which of the following? **(1 mark)**
- **A** the insoluble salt, sodium chloride
- **B** a soluble salt and water
- **C** a neutralisation reaction
- **D** the insoluble salt, barium sulfate

5 Which gas is produced when metals react with acids? **(1 mark)**
- **A** carbon dioxide
- **B** hydrogen
- **C** oxygen
- **D** nitrogen

Score / 5

Short-answer questions

1 Write a balanced symbol equation for the reaction between hydrochloric acid (HCl) and sodium hydroxide (NaOH). **(2 marks)**

2 What would be the products of the reaction between calcium oxide and nitric acid? **(2 marks)**

3 If a salt is formed by a precipitation reaction, how would the salt be separated from the reaction mixture? **(1 mark)**

4 **a)** What type of ions are found in a acid? **(1 mark)**

b) What type of ions are found in an alkali? **(1 mark)**

c) Write the ionic equation for neutralisation reactions, including state symbols. **(3 marks)**

Score / 8

GCSE-style questions

Answer all parts of all questions. Continue on a separate sheet of paper if necessary.

1. Indigestion tablets work by neutralising excess stomach acid. The tablets contain either a base or a carbonate that reacts with the acid, producing a salt and water. If a carbonate is used, carbon dioxide gas is also produced. The effectiveness of different indigestion tablets can be compared by using the apparatus shown.

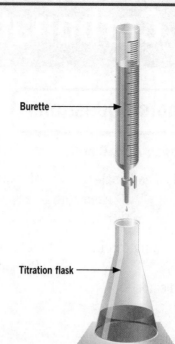

Burette

Titration flask

Ease It

a) To compare two different types of tablet, what would you place in the burette? **(1 mark)**

....

b) Why might it be a good idea to crush the tablets before testing them? **(2 marks)**

....

....

c) What would be placed in the flask in the experiment? **(2 marks)**

....

d) Describe what would be done to compare how well each type of tablet neutralised the acid. **(3 marks)**

....

....

....

e) Apart from how effectively a compound neutralises acid, what other considerations are important in deciding the ingredients of an indigestion tablet? **(2 marks)**

....

....

Score   / 10

Chemistry

How well did you do?

| 0–6 | Try again | 7–13 | Getting there | 14–19 | Good work | 20–25 | Excellent! |

For more information on this topic, see pages 106–107 of your Success Revision Guide.

Metal Carbonate Reactions

Multiple-choice questions

Choose just one answer: A, B, C or D.

1 Which mineral is a carbonate? **(1 mark)**
  A alumina   **B** haematite
  C limestone   **D** rutile

2 Which of the following can be used to test for carbon dioxide? **(1 mark)**
  A Universal indicator
  B litmus paper
  C limewater
  D silver nitrate solution

3 What is the colour change when copper(II) carbonate is heated? **(1 mark)**
  A brown to rust-red   **B** green to black
  C no colour change   **D** white to yellow

4 Which equation represents the reaction between aqueous sodium carbonate and dilute hydrochloric acid? **(1 mark)**
  A $2Na_2CO_3(aq) + 4HCl(aq) \longrightarrow 4NaCl(aq) + 2CO_2(g) + 2H_2(g) + O_2(g)$
  B $2Na_2CO_3(aq) + HCl(aq) \longrightarrow NaHCO_3(aq) + NaCl(aq)$
  C $Na_2CO_3(aq) + 2HCl(aq) \longrightarrow 2NaCl(aq) + CO_2(g) + H_2O(l)$
  D $Na_2CO_3(aq) + 2HCl(aq) \longrightarrow Na_2Cl_2(aq) + CO_2(g) + H_2O(l)$

5 Dilute hydrochloric acid was added to the same mass of each of the following substances. Which substance would produce the graph shown of mass of substance against time? **(1 mark)**

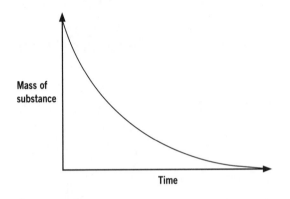

  A copper
  B copper(II) carbonate
  C copper(II) oxide
  D copper(II) sulfate

Score   / 5

Short-answer questions

1 a) Give the name and formula of the salt formed in each of the following reactions.   (10 marks)

Reaction	Name of salt	Formula
sodium carbonate + hydrochloric acid		
magnesium carbonate + sulfuric acid		
zinc carbonate + nitric acid		
calcium carbonate + ethanoic acid		
potassium carbonate + phosphoric acid (H_3PO_4)		

b) Apart from a salt, which TWO other substances are formed in all of the above reactions? (2 marks)

.... and ....

Score   / 12

Answer all parts of all questions. Continue on a separate sheet of paper if necessary.

1 This question is about the preparation of copper(II) sulfate crystals.

a) One spatula full of powdered copper(II) carbonate is added to about $50\,cm^3$ of dilute sulfuric acid. A gas is given off and the mixture gets warm.

   i) What gas is given off? .... (1 mark)

   ii) What name is given to a reaction that gives off heat? .... (1 mark)

   iii) Why is *powdered* copper(II) carbonate used? (1 mark)

   ....

b) Copper(II) carbonate is added until there is no further reaction.

   Give TWO observations that indicate that the reaction has finished.

   i) .... (1 mark)

   ii) .... (1 mark)

c) The mixture is filtered and the filtrate collected in an evaporating basin.

   Why is the mixture filtered? (1 mark)

   ....

d) The filtrate is boiled until it becomes saturated.

   What is the meaning of the following words?

   i) filtrate .... (1 mark)

   ii) saturated .... (1 mark)

e) Crystals form if the filtrate is left in a warm place for several days.

   What has been lost from the evaporating basin during this time? (1 mark)

   ....

f) Write **i)** the word equation and **ii)** the balanced symbol equation, including state symbols, for the above experiment.

   i) .... (1 mark)

   ii) .... (2 marks)

Score   / 12

Chemistry

How well did you do?

| 0–7 | Try again | 8–14 | Getting there | 15–21 | Good work | 22–29 | Excellent! |

For more information on this topic, see pages 108–109 of your Success Revision Guide.

The Electrolysis of Sodium Chloride Solution

Multiple-choice questions

Choose just one answer: A, B, C or D.

1 Which of these is an important use of chlorine? **(1 mark)**
  A flavouring food
  B making bleach
  C making margarine
  D as an industrial alkali

2 What is produced when sodium chloride solution is electrolysed? **(1 mark)**
  A sodium and chlorine only
  B hydrogen and chlorine only
  C chlorine and water only
  D sodium hydroxide, hydrogen and chlorine

3 What happens when sodium chloride solution is electrolysed? **(1 mark)**
  A hydrogen ions are oxidised
  B chloride ions are reduced
  C chloride ions are oxidised
  D sodium ions are reduced

4 When molten lead iodide is electrolysed: **(1 mark)**
  A lead is produced at the cathode
  B iodine is produced at the cathode
  C lead is produced at the anode
  D oxygen is produced at the anode

5 The particles that move when a substance is electrolysed are: **(1 mark)**
  A molecules
  B delocalised electrons
  C ions
  D atoms

Score / 5

Short-answer questions

1 Why is salt spread onto roads in winter? (2 marks)

....

2 When sulfuric acid solution is electrolysed, which two gases are produced? (2 marks)

....

3 Why must lead iodide be heated strongly to allow electrolysis to happen? (2 marks)

....

4 What term describes a reaction where a positive ion gains electrons? (1 mark)

....

5 What term describes a reaction where a negative ion loses electrons? (1 mark)

....

Score / 8

Answer all parts of all questions. Continue on a separate sheet of paper if necessary.

1 This apparatus can be used to electrolyse a solution of sodium chloride in the laboratory. When the current is flowing, bubbles of gas can be seen rising from both electrodes and the electrolyte becomes alkaline. This apparatus is a small-scale version of a major industrial process.

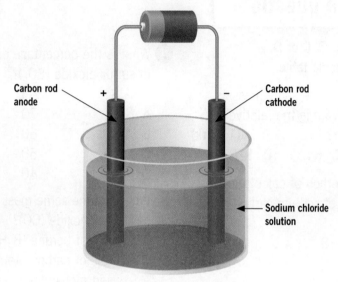

Carbon rod anode +

Carbon rod cathode −

Sodium chloride solution

a) Which TWO gases are produced when sodium chloride is electrolysed? **(2 marks)**

b) What happens to the chloride ions when they reach the positive electrode (anode)? **(2 marks)**

c) Why does the electrolyte become alkaline? **(2 marks)**

d) Write a symbol equation to show the reduction of hydrogen ions at the cathode. **(2 marks)**

e) Give TWO examples of products which use chlorine gas in their manufacture. **(2 marks)**

Score / 10

Chemistry

How well did you do?

0–5 | Try again   6–11 | Getting there   12–17 | Good work   18–23 | Excellent!

For more information on this topic, see pages 110–111 of your Success Revision Guide.

Relative Formula Mass and Percentage Composition

Chemistry

Multiple-choice questions

Choose just one answer: A, B, C or D.
Refer to a copy of the periodic table.

1 Four oxygen atoms have the same mass as one atom of copper. What is the relative atomic mass of copper? **(1 mark)**
A 4   **B** 16   **C** 64   **D** 128

2 What is the correct method of calculating the relative formula mass of sodium carbonate (Na_2CO_3)? **(1 mark)**
A $(2 \times 11) + 6 + 3 \times 8$
B $(2 \times 11) + 6 + 8$
C $(2 \times 23) + 12 + 16$
D $(2 \times 23) + 12 + (3 \times 16)$

3 A compound C_xH_6 has a relative formula mass of 78. What is the value of x? **(1 mark)**
A 2   **B** 3   **C** 6   **D** 12

4 What is the percentage of sulfur and oxygen in sulfur dioxide (SO_2)? **(1 mark)**

	% S	% O
A	30	70
B	40	60
C	50	50
D	60	40

5 What has the same mass as one mole of carbon monoxide (CO)? **(1 mark)**
A 1 mole of borane (B_2H_6)
B 1 mole of carbon atoms + 1 mole of oxygen molecules
C 1 mole of iron atoms
D 1 mole of nitrogen atoms

Score   / 5

Short-answer questions

1 What is meant by the following terms?

a) relative atomic mass .... (2 marks)

b) relative formula (molecular) mass .... (2 marks)

2 This question is about the isotopes of elements in group 7 of the periodic table.

a) i) Bromine forms two isotopes: ^{79}Br and ^{81}Br. The isotopes are equally abundant.
What is the relative atomic mass of naturally occurring bromine? (2 marks)

....

ii) What are the three possible molecular masses of a bromine molecule, Br_2? (3 marks)

.... , ... and ....

b) Chlorine forms two isotopes: ^{35}Cl and ^{37}Cl. Chlorine's relative atomic mass is 35.5, which isotope of chlorine is the most common? Explain your answer. (2 marks)

....

Score   / 11

GCSE-style questions

Answer all parts of all questions. Continue on a separate sheet of paper if necessary.

1 Nitrogen is a very unreactive gas.

a) i) On a separate sheet of paper, draw a diagram of the electronic structure of the nitrogen molecule. **(2 marks)**

ii) With the aid of the diagram, explain why nitrogen is so unreactive. **(2 marks)**

b) Magnesium is a very reactive metal. It burns in nitrogen to form a white solid, Mg_3N_n. Magnesium nitride has the same relative formula mass as calcium carbonate.

i) Show that the relative formula mass of calcium carbonate is 100. **(2 marks)**

ii) What is the value of n in Mg_3N_n? You must show how you calculated the value of n. **(2 marks)**

iii) What is the percentage of magnesium in magnesium nitride? **(2 marks)**

c) When water is added to magnesium nitride a pungent gas is given off that turns damp red litmus paper blue. What gas is given off? **(1 mark)**

d) The other product of the reaction, magnesium hydroxide ($Mg(OH)_2$), is a white solid that is slightly soluble in water. The solution turns red litmus paper blue. What type of compound is magnesium hydroxide? **(1 mark)**

e) 10g of magnesium nitride reacts with water to form 0.30 moles of magnesium hydroxide.

i) Write the word equation for this reaction. **(2 marks)**

ii) How many moles of magnesium nitride is 10g of the substance? **(2 marks)**

iii) From the above information construct the balanced symbol equation, including state symbols, for the reaction between magnesium nitride and water. **(2 marks)**

Score   / 18

How well did you do?

| 0–8 | Try again | 9–16 | Getting there | 17–25 | Good work | 26–34 | Excellent! |

For more information on this topic, see pages 112–113 of your Success Revision Guide.

Chemistry

109

Calculating Masses

Multiple-choice questions

Choose just one answer: A, B, C or D. For questions 2 and 4 refer to the periodic table.

1 When 1 mole of each of the following is completely burnt in oxygen, which one will give the largest mass of carbon dioxide? **(1 mark)**

  A carbon monoxide
  B ethane
  C graphite
  D methane

2 The ionic equation for the reaction between copper and silver nitrate is:

$$Cu(s) + 2Ag^+(aq) \longrightarrow Cu^{2+}(aq) + 2Ag(s)$$

What mass of silver will be formed when 0.2 moles of copper is added to excess silver nitrate? **(1 mark)**

  A 10.8g
  B 12.8g
  C 21.6g
  D 43.2g

3 5.68 g of sodium sulfate (relative formula mass 142) was formed when 10.6 g of sodium carbonate (relative formula mass 106) reacted with excess sulfuric acid.
What was the percentage yield of sodium sulfate? **(1 mark)**

  A 20%   **B** 40%
  C 60%   **D** 80%

4 Zinc reacts with sulfur to form zinc sulfide.

$$Zn(s) + S(s) \longrightarrow ZnS(s)$$

How much zinc sulfide can be made from 6.5 g of zinc? **(1 mark)**

  A 4.6g   **B** 7.8g
  C 8.1g   **D** 9.7g

5 The molecular formula for glucose is $C_6H_{12}O_6$. What is the empirical formula? **(1 mark)**

  A $C_6H_{12}O_6$ **B** CHO
  C CH_2O **D** $CHHO$

Score / 5

Short-answer questions

1 How many moles of the underlined substance are there in each of the following?

  a) When 36.0g of magnesium burns in air, <u>60.0g of magnesium oxide</u> is formed.   (1 mark)

  b) 12.0g of magnesium sulfate reacts with <u>12.6g of water</u>.   (1 mark)

  c) 4g of methane burns to form <u>11g of carbon dioxide</u>.   (1 mark)

  d) <u>10.7g of iron(III) hydroxide</u> is precipitated when excess sodium hydroxide is added to a solution of iron(III) chloride.

      (1 mark)

  e) <u>2.54g of iodine molecules</u> in 250cm³ of water.   (1 mark)

Score / 5

Answer all parts of all questions. Continue on a separate sheet of paper if necessary.

1 When 0.20 moles of a hydrocarbon, G (M_r = 28), was completely burnt in oxygen, 0.40 moles of carbon dioxide was formed.

   a) i) Calculate the number of moles of carbon dioxide formed from 1 mole of G. **(2 marks)**

   ....

   ....

   ii) How many moles of carbon are there in 1 mole of G? .... **(1 mark)**

   b) Hydrocarbon G decolourised bromine water.

   i) In which homologous series is G? **(1 mark)**

   ....

   ii) What is the molecular formula of G? **(1 mark)**

   ....

   iii) Write the balanced symbol equation, including state symbols, for G completely burning in oxygen. **(2 marks)**

   ....

2 The manufacture of nitric acid from ammonia can be represented by this equation:

$$NH_3(g) + 2O_2(g) \longrightarrow HNO_3(g) + H_2O(g)$$

10 moles of ammonia produced 472.5g of nitric acid vapour.

   a) What is the maximum calculated yield of nitric acid that can be produced? **(2 marks)**

   ....

   ....

   b) What is the percentage yield for this reaction? **(2 marks)**

   ....

   ....

   ....

Score   / 11

Chemistry

How well did you do?

| 0–5 | Try again | 6–10 | Getting there | 11–15 | Good work | 16–21 | Excellent! |

For more information on this topic, see pages 114–115 of your Success Revision Guide.

111

Rates of Reaction

Multiple-choice questions

Choose just one answer: A, B, C or D.

1 Which type of reaction is a FAST reaction? **(1 mark)**
- A burning
- B fermenting
- C ripening
- D rusting

2 The rate of a reaction approximately doubles for every 10°C rise in temperature. How much faster is a reaction at 100°C than at 30°C? **(1 mark)**
- A 14 B 32 C 64 D 128

3 Why does the rate of reaction between excess marble chips ($CaCO_3$) and dilute hydrochloric acid slow down? **(1 mark)**
- A all the marble chips have reacted
- B the concentration of the hydrochloric acid decreases
- C the reaction is exothermic
- D the volume of hydrochloric acid decreases

4 Black copper(II) oxide catalyses the decomposition of hydrogen peroxide into water and oxygen. If this experiment was performed, what would you see at the end of the experiment? **(1 mark)**
- A a black solid and a blue solution
- B a black solid and a colourless solution
- C a pink-brown solid and a blue solution
- D a pink-brown solid and a colourless solution

5 What is the effect of increasing the temperature in a chemical reaction? **(1 mark)**
- A increases the rate because the activation energy is lowered
- B increases the rate only if one of the products is soluble in water
- C increases the rate only if the reaction is endothermic
- D increases the rate at which the reactants react

Score / 5

Short-answer questions

1 Choose words from the list below to fill in the gaps in the following passage. Each word should only be used once.

(8 marks)

> activation   catalyst   closer   collisions
> concentration   pressure   surface   temperature

In order for particles to react, they must collide with each other. Only particles with energy greater

than the .... energy will react. This energy can be lowered by using a

.... Reactions can also be speeded up by increasing the energy of the particles by

raising the .... If the reacting particles are made smaller, the .... area

increases and more particles collide. If the reaction involves gases, increasing the ....

increases the rate of reaction. The gas particles are .... together. If the

.... is increased, more particles occupy the same volume and there are more ....

Score / 8

Answer all parts of all questions. Continue on a separate sheet of paper if necessary.

1 Ahmed wanted to find out whether or not copper and copper(II) compounds acted as catalysts in the reaction between zinc and sulfuric acid. In each experiment he used 1.0g of granulated zinc, excess dilute sulfuric acid and 0.1g of the catalyst. He timed how long it took to produce 100 cm³ of hydrogen.

a) On a separate sheet of paper draw a diagram of the apparatus Ahmed could use. Your diagram must show how he kept sulfuric acid and the mixture of zinc powder and catalyst separated before starting the experiment. **(4 marks)**

b) Write the balanced symbol equation, including state symbols, for the reaction between zinc and sulfuric acid. **(2 marks)**

c) How could Ahmed show that hydrogen gas was given off? **(1 marks)**

Here are Ahmed's results:

Catalyst	Time to collect 100 cm³/s	Observations
no catalyst	140	slow reaction
copper(II) sulfate solution	30	pink/brown coloured deposit on zinc, colourless solution
copper(II) chloride	45	pink/brown coloured deposit on zinc, colourless solution
copper powder	54	pink/brown powder left
copper lump	120	pink/brown lump left
copper(II) carbonate	60	gas immediately given off, pink/brown coloured deposit on zinc, light blue solution

d) i) Which substance was acting as the catalyst in this reaction between zinc and sulfuric acid?

.... **(1 mark)**

ii) Why was the first experiment performed without a catalyst? .... **(1 mark)**

iii) What other factor must be kept constant when carrying out these experiments? **(1 mark)**

....

e) Suggest why copper powder is a better catalyst than the lump of copper. **(1 mark)**

Score   / 11

How well did you do?

| 0–6 | Try again | 7–12 | Getting there | 13–18 | Good work | 19–24 | Excellent! |

For more information on this topic, see pages 116–117 of your Success Revision Guide.

113

Chemistry

Reversible Reactions

Multiple-choice questions

Choose just one answer: A, B, C or D.

1 What does the sign $\rightleftharpoons$ indicate about a chemical reaction? **(1 mark)**

A balances
B endothermic
C exothermic
D reversible

2 What can be deduced from the following equation? **(1 mark)**

$$CuSO_4.5H_2O(s) \rightleftharpoons CuSO_4(s) + 5H_2O(l)$$

A the products can be changed back to the reactants
B the reaction can be used as a test for water
C the reaction is endothermic
D there is a colour change from blue to white

3 In which reaction will an increase in pressure, at a constant temperature, favour the formation of products? **(1 mark)**

A $2C(s) + O_2(g) \rightleftharpoons 2CO(g)$
B $2NO(g) + O_2(g) \rightleftharpoons 2NO_2(g)$
C $3Fe(s) + 4H_2O(g) \rightleftharpoons Fe_3O_4(s) + 4H_2(g)$
D $H_2(g) + Br_2(g) \rightleftharpoons 2HBr(g)$

4 The equation for the synthesis of methanol from carbon monoxide and hydrogen in the presence of a copper catalyst is
$$CO(g) + 2H_2(g) \rightleftharpoons CH_3OH(l)$$
exothermic. Which change will NOT affect the equilibrium yield of methanol? **(1 mark)**

A decrease the pressure
B increase the temperature
C increase the amount of catalyst
D increase the size of the reacting vessel

5 Which conditions produce the highest yield of ammonia in the Haber process? **(1 mark)**

	Pressure	Temperature
A	high	high
B	high	low
C	low	high
D	low	low

Score /5

Short-answer questions

1 Fill in the gaps. (7 marks)

Many reactions, such as burning fuel, are irreversible. They go to .... and cannot be

reversed easily. Reversible reactions are where the .... can react to remake the

original .... If the forward reaction is exothermic, the reverse reaction is ....

In the reaction:

ammonium chloride $\rightleftharpoons$ ammonia + hydrogen chloride

ammonium chloride (a white solid) can break down to form .... and ....,

and these can react together to form ....

Score /7

Answer all parts of all questions. Continue on a separate sheet of paper if necessary.

1 The equation below represents the dynamic equilibrium for the hydrolysis of iron(III) chloride.

$$FeCl_3(aq) + 3H_2O(l) \rightleftharpoons Fe(OH)_3(s) + 3HCl(aq)$$

The forward reaction is exothermic.

a) What do you understand by the term 'dynamic equilibrium'? **(2 mark)**

....

....

b) How would you test for the presence of hydrochloric acid in the above equilibrium? **(2 marks)**

....

c) Explain why a precipitate of iron(III) hydroxide disappears when the mixture
is heated. **(3 marks)**

....

....

....

d) Explain why the addition of iron(III) chloride to the heated equilibrium mixture
causes a precipitate of iron(III) hydroxide to reappear. **(2 marks)**

....

....

2 A mixture of the brown gas, nitrogen dioxide, and the pale yellow gas, dinitrogen tetroxide (N_2O_4),
in a closed container is in a state of dynamic equilibrium.

a) Write a balanced symbol equation to show that nitrogen dioxide and dinitrogen
tetroxide are in dynamic equilibrium. **(2 marks)**

....

b) When a corked test tube containing nitrogen dioxide is placed in ice, the colour
changes to pale yellow. If the test tube is placed in warm water, the brown
colour is restored. Explain these observations. **(2 marks)**

....

....

....

Score / 13

How well did you do?

| 0–4 | Try again | 5–9 | Getting there | 10–18 | Good work | 19–25 | Excellent! |

For more information on this topic, see pages 118–119 of your Success Revision Guide.

Chemistry

Energy Changes

Multiple-choice questions

Choose just one answer: A, B, C or D.

1 Measuring heat energy changes is called: **(1 mark)**
   - **A** thermochemistry
   - **B** kinetics
   - **C** cryogenics
   - **D** calorimetry

2 What is the specific heat capacity of water usually given as? **(1 mark)**
   - **A** 4.18 °C
   - **B** 4.18 kJ/mol
   - **C** 4.18 J/g/°C
   - **D** 4.18 kcal

3 What is the best way to work out the heat energy produced by the fuel in a spirit burner? **(1 mark)**
   - **A** measure the temperature change in the fuel
   - **B** measure the temperature change in a measured volume of water
   - **C** measure the temperature change in the surrounding air
   - **D** measure the mass change in a measured volume of water

4 Which of these would make a simple calorimeter for a neutralisation reaction? **(1 mark)**
   - **A** a polystyrene cup with a lid
   - **B** a metal beaker
   - **C** a glass beaker
   - **D** a test tube with a tight-fitting bung

Score   / 4

Short-answer questions

1 When comparing the heat energy released by burning different liquid fuels in a spirit burner, how can the mass of fuel burned be calculated? **(2 marks)**

2 What two measurements must be taken to determine the temperature change of a known mass of water? **(1 mark)**

3 Why is it important that a calorimeter is as well-insulated as possible? **(2 marks)**

4 How can we know the mass of a measured volume of water without actually weighing it? **(2 marks)**

5 To calculate the energy change for a neutralisation reaction, 25 cm³ of 1 mol/dm³ sodium hydroxide solution is mixed with 25 cm³ of 1 mol/dm³ hydrochloric acid in a calorimeter. What is the mass of water that has been heated? **(2 marks)**

Score   / 9

GCSE-style questions

Answer all parts of all questions. Continue on a separate sheet of paper if necessary.

1 A student was comparing the energy released by burning different alcohols. For each fuel, she used a spirit burner, weighing the burner before and after the burning. The fuel was burned for 5 minutes underneath a copper beaker containing $100\,cm^3$ of water. The temperature change in the water was measured and she was able to calculate the energy given out for each fuel, in kJ/g. Here are her results:

Alcohol	Formula	Energy released (kJ/g)
methanol	CH_3OH	22.7
ethanol	C_2H_5OH	29.7
propanol	C_3H_7OH	33.7
butanol	C_4H_9OH	36.1
pentanol	$C_5H_{11}OH$	35.8

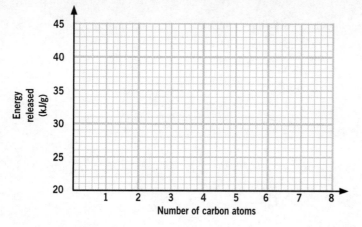

a) Plot the results for the experiments as a line graph on the axes, adding a line of best fit to show the pattern. **(2 marks)**

b) One of the results is anomalous. Draw a circle around the anomalous result. **(1 mark)**

c) Describe the pattern shown by the results of the experiments. **(2 marks)**

....

d) Use the graph to predict the energy that would be released by burning 1.0 g of

hexanol, $C_6H_{13}OH$ .... **(1 mark)**

e) The student noticed, after burning pentanol, that there was soot on the outside of the copper beaker. How had soot been made in the reaction? **(2 marks)**

....

Score / 8

How well did you do?

| 0–5 | Try again | | 6–10 | Getting there | | 11–15 | Good work | | 16–21 | Excellent! |

For more information on this topic, see pages 120–121 of your Success Revision Guide.

117

Notes

Notes

Periodic Table

Key

relative atomic mass
atomic symbol
name
atomic (proton) number

	Group																
	1	2											3	4	5	6	7	0

1 **H** hydrogen 1		

1	2											3	4	5	6	7	0
																	4 **He** helium 2
7 **Li** lithium 3	9 **Be** beryllium 4											11 **B** boron 5	12 **C** carbon 6	14 **N** nitrogen 7	16 **O** oxygen 8	19 **F** fluorine 9	20 **Ne** neon 10
23 **Na** sodium 11	24 **Mg** magnesium 12											27 **Al** aluminium 13	28 **Si** silicon 14	31 **P** phosphorus 15	32 **S** sulfur 16	35.5 **Cl** chlorine 17	40 **Ar** argon 18
39 **K** potassium 19	40 **Ca** calcium 20	45 **Sc** scandium 21	48 **Ti** titanium 22	51 **V** vanadium 23	52 **Cr** chromium 24	55 **Mn** manganese 25	56 **Fe** iron 26	59 **Co** cobalt 27	59 **Ni** nickel 28	63.5 **Cu** copper 29	65 **Zn** zinc 30	70 **Ga** gallium 31	73 **Ge** germanium 32	75 **As** arsenic 33	79 **Se** selenium 34	80 **Br** bromine 35	84 **Kr** krypton 36
85 **Rb** rubidium 37	88 **Sr** strontium 38	89 **Y** yttrium 39	91 **Zr** zirconium 40	93 **Nb** niobium 41	96 **Mo** molybdenum 42	[98] **Tc** technetium 43	101 **Ru** ruthenium 44	103 **Rh** rhodium 45	106 **Pd** palladium 46	108 **Ag** silver 47	112 **Cd** cadmium 48	115 **In** indium 49	119 **Sn** tin 50	122 **Sb** antimony 51	128 **Te** tellurium 52	127 **I** iodine 53	131 **Xe** xenon 54
133 **Cs** caesium 55	137 **Ba** barium 56	139 **La*** lanthanum 57	178 **Hf** hafnium 72	181 **Ta** tantalum 73	184 **W** tungsten 74	186 **Re** rhenium 75	190 **Os** osmium 76	192 **Ir** iridium 77	195 **Pt** platinum 78	197 **Au** gold 79	201 **Hg** mercury 80	204 **Tl** thallium 81	207 **Pb** lead 82	209 **Bi** bismuth 83	[209] **Po** polonium 84	[210] **At** astatine 85	[222] **Rn** radon 86
[223] **Fr** francium 87	[226] **Ra** radium 88	[227] **Ac*** actinium 89	[261] **Rf** rutherfordium 104	[262] **Db** dubnium 105	[266] **Sg** seaborgium 106	[264] **Bh** bohrium 107	[277] **Hs** hassium 108	[268] **Mt** meitnerium 109	[271] **Ds** darmstadtium 110	[272] **Rg** roentgenium 111							

Elements with atomic numbers 112–116 have been reported but not fully authenticated

*The lanthanoids (atomic numbers 58–71) and the actinoids (atomic numbers 90–103) have been omitted.

The relative atomic masses of copper and chlorine have not been rounded to the nearest whole number.